Duet in the Little Blue Church

Books by Sharon Chmielarz

Different Arrangements

But I Won't Go Out in a Boat

Stranger in Her House

The Other Mozart

The Rhubarb King

Calling

The Sky Is Great the Sky Is Blue

Love from the Yellowstone Trail

Visibility: Ten Miles, a Prairie Memoir in Photography and Poetry

The Widow's House

little eternities

The J Horoscope

Speaking in Riddles

The Pied Piper of Hamelin

The End of Winter

Down at Angel's

Duet in the Little Blue Church

poems new and selected

Sharon Chmielarz

NODIN PRESS

Copyright © 2023 by Sharon Chmielarz, all rights reserved. For permission to reproduce selections from this book and to learn more about Nodin Press, visit www.nodinpress.com.

Cover photo credit: Kenneth Smith. The Berlin Baptist Church. "The church being set above the plowed fields and poking just over the horizon gives it an interesting layered look. The dust off to the side suggests farm activity. The furrows suggest reliance on the dirt and hope for growth."

ISBN: 978-1-947237-52-0

9 8 7 6 5 4 3 2 1

Library of Congress Control Number: 2023931650

Published by
Nodin Press
210 Edge Place
Minneapolis, MN   55418
www.nodinpress.com

Printed in U.S.A.

to heart, mind, friendship

Dear Reader,

First of all, thank you for your interest in this book. It represents the fourteen books of poetry I've had published over the past four decades. When I began writing, in my mid-thirties, poet Michael Dennis Browne observed that most of my poems were about birds. Could I maybe try other subjects. Like what. Well, there's family. Family?! I'd been running from them all my life! —*Duet in the Little Blue Church* records poems about places and people where I stopped to listen.

Themes surfaced book by book: from the Ur theme of a troubled, working class family life to a keen interest in other women's lives; daughter and father relationships; history; widowhood; time's flexibility; stories and understandings that disguised my original confessional style. *Duet's* ... fulcrum is a section of poems from multiple books about the prairie where I was raised. My relationship to my own father is/ was possibly the major impetus that first drove me to write.

I hope that *Duet in the Little Blue Church* works not only as an engaging poetry collection but also as an autobiographical record of one midwestern woman and her writing life, first learning craft as a late-starter, then developing and strengthening hopefully her style, voice, and interests in poetry's multiple leeways.

Sharon

Contents

New Poems

We Missed the Boat / 5
Stoves Go Well with Snow / 7
Eight South Dakota Riffs on
Rilke's "Herbsttag" (Autumn Day) / 8
City of Arhirit / 11
Five x Five Equals Two Fives / 12
The Old Woman in a Time of Aggression / 13
Prayers like Good Samaritans / 14
The Present Gives Up Some Past / 15
Photo of a Friend's Marsh in Winter / 16
Earthly Home / 17
Re the Tree Outside My Sink Window: Winter Spaces / 18
Ella's Pies / 19
The Traveler / 21
At the People's Bakery / 22
Could I Ever Write a Poem Like His / 24
Aunt B / 25
Doesn't It Swell / 26
The Robin's Wife / 27
To Put My Finger on It / 28
Waking at Night / 29
Notes on a Bedside Pad / 30
About the Very Few Sightings of
Jaguars in the Wild … / 31

Different Arrangements (1982)

Old Lines / 35
Near the Iris / 36
Night Out with Mom / 37
In Conversation with Gertrude Stein / 38
At the Banquet to Honor Rousseau / 40

The Poet's Double / 41
Snake / 42

BUT I WON'T GO OUT IN A BOAT (1991)

Do Not Disturb / 45
Like a Church / 46
Homecoming / 47
Taking a Snow Bath / 48
Playing His Heart Out / 49
Rabbit / 50
During the Blizzard / 51
They Come Humming / 52

STRANGER IN HER HOUSE (1995)

On My Mother's Death: Harvesting / 55
In His Hands / 56
Reins / 57

THE OTHER MOZART (2001)

All I Want / 61
Between Art and Usefulness / 62
Nannerl Mozart: Speaking of Her Retirement / 63
Nannerl Mozart: Fashioning a Single Response / 64
Nannerl Mozart on Names: Trazom / 65
Leopold Mozart : On the Cross / 66
Pros & Cons: A Marriage of Convenience /67
Winter of 1784-85 / 68
The Glass Lady / 69
A Blue Note / 70
Playing Four Hands with Wolfgang / 71
The Visit / 72

The Rhubarb King (2006)

The Rhubarb King / 77
Washing My Face / 79
Rooms / 80
Remembering the Acts Done to the Dead / 81
In a Russian Garden / 83
Duet in a Little Blue Church / 84
Hands / 85
In His Car / 86
The Old Man Makes It / 87
Watching Two Crows Circle / 88

Calling (2010)

Portraits of Sister Maria Celeste, Daughter
to Galileo Galilei, a Poem in Fourteen Sayings / 91
On the Train to Milan, the Conductor, il Controllare /99
The Bürgermeister's Wife's Account / 102
The Skatplayer's Tale / 103
The Last Queen of France / 105
Monet's Egg Girl / 106
Stalin's Daughter / 108
Three Faces / 109
Akhmatova's Place / 110
Pictures of an Extinction: The Motherland / 111
Mrs. Heinike and Mr. Mendelssohn / 114
Dog Days at Court / 115
On Brothers: A Conversation Between Dorothy
Wordsworth and Nannerl Mozart in the Afterlife / 118
Music, I Must Have Music / 119
Subjects / 122
A Christmas Story ... of a Sort / 125

"Dear Little Sister"–Wil van Gogh / 126
Wonder Woman at Seventy / 127
The Bird Men / 128

The Sky Is Great, the Sky Is Blue (2010)

Along the Wall, *Jakuba ul* / 133
Garden Scene / 134
Bells / 135
Tomatoes / 136
An Evening of Klezmer / 137
The Vistula / 138
Pattern / 139

On the Prairie

Selections from *Love from the Yellowstone Trail* (2013); *Visibility Ten Miles: A Prairie Memoir in Photography and Poetry* (2015); *The Sky Is Great, the Sky Is Blue* (2010)

First a River / 143
Fire and Water / 145
Love from the Yellowstone Trail / 148
Old Glory Passes By / 150
McIntosh, South Dakota / 153
Two Voices from the Trail / 154
In Each Other's Hair / 155
Lucifer at the Supper Table / 156
Notes from the Trail / 157
Variations on Water / 161
Milton on the Plains / 162
Another Love Letter / 163
Now It's Late / 164
Fruit Closet / 165
In Ascent / 166
How Do We Live in Winter Without Zinnias? / 167

Mr. Schmier's Wife / 168
Wax Cylinder Recordings from a Small Town / 169
View from Porch / 174
Burning / 175
The Beekeepers / 176
Wounded Knee / 178
Haying / 179
The Accent on Flat / 180
Lilacs / 181
New Water / 182
Zippers / 183
Everything / 184

THE WIDOW'S HOUSE (2016)

Soon You're Free / 187
At His Bedside / 189
Talk / 190
Tastes / 191
A Widow's Tale / 197
Elegy in a Single Bed / 198
The Bottom Rung on the Social Ladder (Well, Just Above Bingo): Watching Love Movies on a Friday Night, Alone / 199
Purgatory / 201
Goodnight / 202
On Green / 203
Fishers Club / 205
Chance / 206
Once Late on a December Afternoon / 207

LITTLE ETERNITIES (2017)

Time Traveler / 211
Summer of 2013 / 212
If I Bend to Pick You Up / 214

I Won't Turn on the Radio / 215
Size / 216
Thyme / 218
L'Arlésienne: Madame Joseph-Michel Ginoux / 219
Eye Hole / 220
On Milton's Political Pamphlets and the Measure of Time / 221
The Tsarina's Tea Set / 222
A Life with the Movies / 223
One Has to Say / 224
For the Millions Who Were Starved to Death in Ukraine / 225
The 900 Pound Man, the Fattest in the World / 226
The Wounded Angel / 228
Re: The Art of Painting, *De Schilderkonst* / 229
A Small Repast of Tea and Kippers / 230
Mr. Miłosz, Aprés Party / 231
Starry Nights of Pantry Labor / 232
185. Little Eternities / 233

THE J HOROSCOPE (2019)

Intersection #1 / 237
Yahweh the Stork / 238
The Boatman's Wife / 239
The Cuckold's Dream / 241
Luck Out for a Walk / 242
Dove with Hint of Green Backs / 243
These Earthlings May Have Seen Yahweh / 244
Ms. Yahweh in P.S. #1 / 246
Flies, Theology 1. & Flies, Theology 2 ./ 267
Intersection #8 / 248
The Family Album / 249
Yahweh the Stork re Mother One Heart / 250
To Joseph the Dreamer, the Pretty Boy / 251
Intersection #6 / 255

Lost in Love / 256
The Gardiner in Eden / 257
Yahweh the Cook's Opinion / 258
Eve's Daughter Marilyn / 259
Cain / 260
The First Woman to Have an Egg Planted
Between Her Legs / 261
Yahweh the Avenger / 262
Yahweh the Rock / 263
Where One Becomes Two / 264
Yahweh the Stork Re a Human Condition / 265
The Host / 266

SPEAKING IN RIDDLES (2021)

Seven Riddles / 271
Solutions to Riddles 273

Acknowledgments / 275
About the Author / 277

Duet in the Little Blue Church

New Poems

"Being alone is no way to be: thus
loneliness is the test of pure being."

"Wicht," Stanley Plumly, Poetry, June, 2019

We Missed the Boat

    after the children's book Brave Irene by William Steig; for T.

Never compare yourself to another,
especially when she's Irene Bobbin
at the door to her mother's little yellow
parlor with its pictures and mannequin.
"Bye! I'll deliver the gown to the Duchess."

Mrs. Bobbin, a single mom, brimming
with exhaustion, called from her bed,
"Don't go, Irene, a storm is brewing."
But Irene set off with gown in box,
into the darkening winter afternoon.

(You and I set out, too, on a mission.)

Even though the wind tore open the box,
even though the snow was hip high,
even though Irene thought she was lost,
maybe going in circles,
she struggled on.

(Did we quit too early?)

Somewhere past Farmer Bennett's pasture
the wind was so strong, it blew away
two tissue-paper ghosts that sheltered
the beautiful pink, sparkly dress.
And the dress, too.

(What went wrong for us?)

Irene had a mission for sure.
She was focused on succeeding,
a matter of food for the cupboards,

wood for her mother's cold stove,
and something for the pot on it.

(We could've tried harder, I guess.)

Irene's tasks doubled. Now she must
find the lost gown. In rough, gangly,
primordial woods where there's no
sense of direction, she stumbled on,
snow blind, from tree

to tree, until her little legs protested
they could lift themselves no more.
But there! At wit's end, there was
the dress, plastered to a tree,
decking the trunk out for a party.

(Maybe the Fates were against us.)

A sight indeed for sore eyes.
And not much farther on, an amber
window light spilled out over the snow.
The palace! Irene huddled before the door.
Like a snow sculpture, but she'd made it!

(And if she hadn't? That happens, too.)

All good things followed. The Duchess's
pleasure over the gown, the warm ballroom,
the delicious feast an absolute joy
for porridge-fed Irene. And best of all
a purse full of money for her mom. The end.

(It almost hurts, others' triumphs, they feel so good.)

Stoves Go Well with Snow

> for Ella

It's snowing. For snow, heatedly.
Inside the four-room house, in the realm
of kitchen, the faithful stove is a Crisco
white-clothed nurse. Stout. The back
door opens and someone, stomping snow
from their boots, lets the cold in.

The stove is a step up from the former,
smelly, dangerous kerosene. It's an electric
therapist on a blizzardy day, the calmer-
downer, warmer-upper, scented goodness,
roasted tenderness. Good ol' stove, good
ol' oven. Queen of peace. Ear and register.

Untraveled, stove's at home in its cave
between cabinet and wall. Wordless, it's
dependent on sense of smell/ taste/ touch/
maybe Jesus/ to deliver us from thoughts
in the house. Sometimes. Sometimes,
Burn baby burn I don't give a shit.

Turned on,
stove is the only real savior
in the house. It can hold its breath
at 350º
for two or more hours. Amazing lungs.
Amazing heart.

Eight South Dakota Riffs on Rilke's "Herbsttag" (Autumn Day)

"Herr, es ist Zeit, der Sommer war sehr gross, ..."

1.
You up there! Time-turner! It's time.
Open your hands, loosen the winds,
clear the skies. Make sure, make sure
there's more heart than anger in your
long shadows, that the sundial's style
shows it's time to sweeten dark red
melancholic wines. Let field machine
headlights scour rows of corn like prowling
bot-suns in the night. Entrust our hands—
the drivers, rakers, washers and fillers
of jars and bottles. And the harvest's bins.

2.
A day begins. Shadows—
the furrow's,
the combine's,
the farmer's,
and morning's
on elongated legs—
bob toward the fields.

3.
It's time, dew has vanished from the field.
Midmorning, dry wheat stands up nice
and straight before the combine's header,
the cutter, the gatherer, feeding the combine.
And from this beginning, a yellow arc of grain—
a spray of gold—shoots out into the grain cart.
Commodity on the grain exchange.
Maybe 50, 70 bushels an acre. To finish
all a farmer needs is a steady south wind
bringing in a few more sunny days.

4.
Following time
the sundial's style
moves by shadow,
pointing to the hour,
each one an ending
or beginning.
Whatever the wind.
Whatever the weather.

5.
O moon-y heaviness in the word
autumnal, its drum beat sound
      au tum nal.
O time of tree frogs' chirping
rings around evening.
      Au tum nal.

6.
A small house. An easy chair,
so comfy to collapse into
in the living room,
in sunlight, in faint
November sunlight.
Whoever hasn't a house now …
Wer jetzt kein Haus hat …

7.
Out walking fall evenings a man or woman
learns a lane's moves, slopes, shadows.
Aimlessness for those who have no field,
no work, no stoop to sweep, nothing grown
by the bushel. Ahead, accumulation of time.

Who am I but an arrogant hiker, a rogue soul,
too smart for faith but still admiring the magic
in fallen, smoldering leaves. This is my right.

Like the right of sun to burn its hot sure threat—
Hurry Hurry—to the field's ingredients for bread.

8.
After an autumn rain, the sky's a fast-moving
clock of ever-changing clouds. Cottonwoods
turn wet streets golden with their fallen leaves.
East of town, husks blown from a cornfield's
rows of blond-gray stocks fly across your
windshield. Like singles from flocks of pale-
feathered birds, they swirl about as if they were
on their way up, up into air's atrium.

City of Arhirit

1976, photograph by James Turrell

Was it founded to be happy,
somewhere in Morocco,
or maybe Spain?

Perspective
leads past a street
corner to the narrow

hallway all old lanes
turn into.
At the end, light

makes a red border
around a closed door.
The air

is so dense
breathing turns
into midnight.

FIVE x FIVE EQUALS TWO-FIVE

When we're lonely we may feel peculiarly
close to odd details, old details sliding
way back to the Goths who lost fingers
left and right whetting their axes
or butchering wild boars that bit
off the bird-finger, doomed to spend
the rest of its days apart from the hand.
Which is always at its most handsome
with all digits accounted for. Was it too
much to expect to keep two fives, even
in hardscrabble times?
                                  Guessing
now—the Goth word for "five" was finf?
Halfway between fünf and *five* as in toes,
or where Galileo deduced a system's number
of moons and comets. In addition he had three
children. His bastard son married into money,
the two daughters died in their teens in a convent.
Their mother, the housekeeper, married.
From five down to two: Galileo the odd
man out with his telescope. Under a welter
of suns maybe he was the lonesome one.

The Old Woman in a Time of Aggression

I do not want to end my days in a closet
of a room, my bed piled high with blankets
and a floor rug to keep warm.
But here I am. A neighbor of the kind sort
brings me gruel or tea from staples
she's stashed in her cupboard. My rescue
then is memory of the plentiful times,
plenty being little but more. And will
the relatives and friends around me, my
ghosts, be happy in my flimsy remembrances?
Flimsy times and flimsy houses in my head?
What if someone comes along and robs me,
and the last of the spuds I hid away, gone
from the drawer. With salt, my fine supper.
I'll chip some ice from the windowsill.
I'll make myself a cup of cold water.
My happiness! Who'll rob me of that.

My happiness! Who'll rob me of that.
I'll make myself a cup of cold water.
I'll chip some ice from the windowsill.
With salt, my fine supper in a drawer
is the last of the spuds I hid away. But what
if someone comes along and robs me?
Flimsy times and flimsy houses in my head,
ghosts happy in my flimsy remembrances,
the relatives and friends around me, my
plenty being little but more. And will
then memory of the plentiful times be
stashed away in my cupboard? A rescuer
bringing me gruel or tea from staples.
But here I am. A neighbor of the kind sort,
with a floor rug to keep me warm, my bed
piled high with blankets for my room.
I do not want to end my days in a closet.

Prayers Like Good Samaritans

I don't know about prayers. What's the time limit on answers
during the upwards-downwards flow from their bulging clouds?

Unharnessed in space, taking skyways sideways, maybe prayers
streak in Super-Shuttle-blue coursing over freeways.

Airborne delivery's slow, hit and miss, could even land in
the wrong century. There's no invoice, no returns. No C.O.D.

Over thousands of years are replies mere templates—to an affair,
Answer 1; danger of war, Answer 2; Joy, etc., Answer 3. Or?

I know of a man who prayed sixteen times a day, a human telegraph
tapping into the ether, his prayers as intimate and burning as stars—

waiting.

The Present Gives Up Some Past

She can't shake it: This hour picked out like a dress
that fits her and she looks nice in it or even very
nice as her husband might say. She's troweling
into comfort soil, digging a hole for roots,
the lilies' she found growing in a ditch.
She drove back with a spade for this bunch.
The yard's mapped-out directions tuck traffic
noise away–the vehicular and emotional.
The lilies' yellow, a choice color, is a real flourish,
as is her cat's sudden appearance from somewhere–
the locust or scaly apple tree, the purple maple,
the three elms, green-bearded lords at the border
to the neighbor's apple orchard. The cat's fur,
the leaves, warm, lit by sunlight's blur.

Sounds rolling out the patio door: grocery sacks
rustling in the kitchen. Her husband. Imagine!
She had a husband then, and he's returned.
Anybody home? His former German accent barely
detectable. *Just wondering where everybody is.*
The cat's already racing up the deck steps. The woman
pats the soil down around the lilies and waters them.
Satisfied, she slaps loose soil from her hands and
joins her two everybody-home-agains in the kitchen.

Photo of a Friend's Marsh in Winter

for Joyce Sutphen

An uncut field of cattails in old bone yellow,

born into growth, as if patient in the cold.

Maybe a representation of center stage

loneliness, a peculiar state of being

alive but not; dead, but not. Maybe

a consideration of insular navigation,

reeds without red-winged blackbirds.

Enter stage left: a doe, ears alert,

and her yearling; their part, a tentative

stepping out, counterpart to motion.

Hooves in snow, the foragers have arrived.

Their time here will be brief. It's

an age-old plot on earth, to have little

time to search and find before dusk falls.

Earthly Home

after the poem "Adelstrop," Edward Thomas, 1878-1917

Yes, I remember the garden–
spaded by hand, seedlings started by hand.
Tomatoes and green peppers gorged on full sun
scenting rows familiar with hose and hoe.

Before anyone else was awake I was
making my breakfast from a row of carrots.
Beet leaves squatted in dew at my feet.
The air, savory from the volunteer dill.

August! a swatch of time, untidy, frilly,
straggly vines and stems, plumped-up-crazy-
rich tomatoes, and on and over dirt foot paths
hungry potato bugs, a garter snake, and bees.

Around the garden, a homemade fence.
On the west, neighbor Molstads' yard.
Past their apple tree and Railroad Avenue, then
train wheel rumble and the Missouri's shadowed hills.

Re the Tree Outside My Sink Window: Winter Spaces

Georg Segal, "Walking Man," 1988

The tree is
on its way
to bones and marrow

like a statue,
George Segal's
man in trench coat,

rain plastering
his coat and hair,
he who is everyman

lifts his face
to the wet
decency of sorrow.

Ella's Pies

1.
Roll the dough out. Stretch it over the pie plate.
Thumb thumb all around the pie plate's rim.
If the crust tears, roll it up and do it over again,
belly bound to the kitchen counter.
For how many hours? —Let us count.

2.
At least two pies a week, winter or summer.
Add five extra pies at holidays=15.
Subtract pies baked for church dinners =0.
Sum so far, 52x2=104 +15=119 per year.
At one hour per pie, round this out
to 120 hours x 1945 to 1995=50 years,*
if my math is correct=one year?

> *I didn't count Depression years.
> Extra flour and lard were rare.

My mother spent one year of her life baking pies?
Only one year? Why does her sentence
seem longer? Like 8765.82 years?*
Does the opposite, happiness, weigh in
then in seconds? Fast flying? Uncommon?

> *525,949.2 minutes in a year, Siri tells me,
> and 8765.82 hours per year.

How much was Ella paid,
she in the panthéon of pie makers,
the world of "it smells good in here."
By the hour, pie, year, or second.
Consider the possibilities. It may be A
or B, C or D or All of the Above.
Ha! Trick question. Ella the pie baker,
who lives in the House of Zeus, sweats
without pay. Answer: Zero is Zero.

3.
Minnesota Betty—*Betty's Pies* on Highway 61—
a familiar location for every North Shore tourist—
pays her crew by the hour and/ or by the pie,
wages figured into the pie's price.
We all expect that. No free lunch; no free pie.
I wonder how much Betty makes a year.
It's been years since I've wanted pie. Or made one.

4.
You know how hours go by—fleet as an Audi
on the open road or stalled beside a highway
in Missouri. So learn addition. Develop a good
nose. One thing pie makers know in their blood
and won't find in a cookbook: Get up early
in summer, bake when the house is coolest.
Cool down Zeus* with pie for evening dessert.

*Those seconds, their hour gentles my father.

5.
Apple, banana, raisin, prune, mince meat,
lemon meringue, pumpkin, and peach.

Ella! Where are you? —*Here, Lord,*
sliding a pie into the oven. *I'll have*

just a sliver of each. Light. Warmth.
Life. African violet on the windowsill.

The Traveler

For her, a dinner—
lobster on a platter.
Out there, the harbor,
little boats skirt the bar.

She of the daily planner,
the yellow highlighter,
the eye upon the hour,
relaxes in her chair.

She the runner, earlier
the jogger along the shore,
its gray sand softer
than pavers, like wet powder

underfoot. She the outsider
taking on the air
of a beachfront insider,
finding in the sea desire.

Oh yes, the darker, fuller
heart beats faster, her
heart like the weather,
her lips warmed by butter.

At the People's Bakery

The counter's bread basket sits marvelously empty.
The People are buying designer breads!
One opened-mouth asks, Any more with flax seed?
The baker prances to the oven door.

The People are buying designer breads!
Brinnng goes the bell, the oven door's unlatched.
The baker prances in the opened oven's heat.
She flicks her fingers. Ouch! Hot designers.

When the bell goes Brinnng the oven's unlatched.
Love for loaves shines in the people's eyes.
The baker flicks her fingers. (Hot designers.)
Ouch! She slips a loaf into a paper sack.

Love for loaves shines in the people's eyes.
The baker is paid to be burned and be patient
slipping a loaf into a brown paper sack.
An oven-ly fragrance floats up from the sack.

The baker is paid to be burned but *Hey! Be patient!*
The people's bread must stand up to the knife.
An oven-ly fragrance swoons 'round the sacks
of bread that won't sag and stick when sliced.

The people's bread stands up to the knife.
This. is. my. breadbasket. the baker sings. She
pats her belly for bread that won't sag and stick.
Who wants to eat a tortured slice?

This. is. my. breadbasket. the baker sings
to the people's bread and their bellies.
Who wants to eat a tortured slice
all saggy and sticky in the mouth? —Why

the People are buying designer breads.
The counter's bread basket sits marvelously empty.
The baker prances before the oven door.
One opened-mouth asks, Any more with flax seed?

Could I Ever Write a Poem Like His

after"I Could Never Write a Poem to This City":Alfredo Zaldívar

May I sing with you, Black cowboy,
your hat and buckle

like your bass guitar
named Trouble Here and Gone,
Gone but Here

like a match box on fire, rhythm
and tone torched

like your knobbed and knolly
fingertips coaxing strings
to give it up

like your left foot lives
by itself in the beat

and your opened shirt
shows neck down to chest
where your gold necklace rocks

to the clef in the cleft,
the chain, a pendulum

damp from your skin's
brown suede. Like your
song is not for touching

you, your song,
not for my possession.

Aunt B

In autumn the summerhouse door she shoved
open landed her in a stuffy room, soon to
swarm in sugar steam from scalded jars:
the annual canning, putting up—Aunt B
heating up the canner's water on the old stove.

On August's agenda—crab apples. Hers from
trees not grafted to bear miniature inedibles
but troves of reds and yellows guarded from
bird pillage and savored as the ingredient
for sauce when a woman lives in the same place

all her life. Like her you'd notice, too, the fields
getting so they were all lakes and marshes.
You'd be happy, too, when women could wear
pants on the tractor or at work with the header.
That was *hardt* in a dress, Aunt B huffed.

When company stopped by she served sauce.
Crabapple sauce. With a square of cake.
Like her mother. And now her daughter-in-law.
The apple, says the proverb, doesn't fall far
Der Apfel fällt nicht weit ... from the tree.

Doesn't It Swell

The crabtree's petals, done in by a stormy weekend,
reveal galaxies of tiny, pink, five-pointed calyxes
poking out among the leaves. This phase won't last long,
and won't bring the tree's boughs down shapeless
as the woman who bore eighteen children.

Today I count twenty-three buds slowly opening
on the young pink peony. I don't need them—
or do I—yet I want them to swell and bloom
in my garden. Over the petaled grass, broken
egg shells rest, but no yolk smear. Signs:

Friends! The future will fill with robin trill.
Full! The way I feel some days
when I have no trouble living with myself.

The Robin's Wife

She lives in the house beside a crabapple tree,
the tree she loves, a snow-caked crab tree.
Wind gusts through, and the white stuff
swirls from the boughs at the mercy of wind
and the many grays of February, the color
of listlessness and her husband's passing.

Morning's inhabited by silence, an estate
of cold. Beyond Cold. Sun-dogs out.
Movement making an appearance outside
her window is everything—there—a robin.
Plumped up orange breast is his buffer
and flag. The weight of him, lean bone
and feather. His tail shivers; it isn't a flit.
In a landscape offering extinction, intrepid
of him to call out. So they pass cold time.

To Put My Finger on It

I once tried sketching the elm in our front yard.
(It guarded the driveway, you wouldn't have wanted
to crash into its trunk.) Lounging on our deck,
tablet in hand, I got lost in the tree's branches,
uncountable roads of joints and junctures.

My paper elm was a destitute approximation.
Next I tried making an apple, oh, so much more
than red. My crayon box—unable to assist.
And what if the apple had been capped in snow,
blue and gray morsels of tints, their light?

I gave up apples for clouds, letting my arm roll
into billowing. Is art about possession? admiration?
Constable's cumulus explosions, Turner's pale
yellow interiors, Constable's mist, Turner's steaminess?
They are so beyond my glance-fulls.

Sat and looked then. Clouds rarely speak
in first person singular. That one there
looks like a young woman mothering an old.
Others are more stage-y. Sets. Walk-ons. Lucky
hills step right up sometimes to join the clouds.

Waking at Night

Such a short distance between genius
   and shit. Take those elephant turds
      Bruce Conner (1991 Walker Art Center)
         stacked in piles on the floor, soft cannon balls,
            so appealing to some humans, something we can

all relate to. In my claustrophobic tiny corner
   (compared to the Milky Way) I am happy,
      moon-devotée that I am, when a rag of the ancient
         floats first hand outside my window.–Take
            these lines I've scribbled in the darkness around

my bed. I hope they don't entwine,
   as illegible by daylight as barbed wire
      some French girls stood behind,
         on display at the end of a war,
            brunette and blond collaborators

whose hair was shorn, cut off for bedding-up
   with Wehrmacht men who gave them cognac
      and nylons they could sell on the black market
         for bread. They were cross-and-bones thin, all
            skull, spat upon, reviled little female

christs.–*It's just dizziness. It'll pass. It's just this*
   time of night and the room so small. There
      are bad dreams and then it's over and they/
         we/ I can go back to sleep again.
            But why would anybody

pilfer feces from the elephant kings?
   Reverence? Even elephant spirit-
      eyes pop seeing their dung
         bargained off alongside
            their ivory tusks.

Notes on a Bedside Pad

Is all of life, age then? Passing from one generation to another?
Here you are watching a ten-year-old sail his boat
across the pond in the Garden of Luxembourg.
Here you are, phone in hand, standing boggled
in the stout court of Heinrich *der Löwe*, the lion.
Symbol of Bavarian strength, he lived in 1142.
Ur-lions never needed statues in the Serengeti,
which sounds so much like the word 'spaghetti'
that young and old mouths begin to water.

Is all of life relevance? A field before the hail storm?
The lucky fields of wheat, young and growing in Tuscany
for pasta are excellent, and yet compared to the wheat
in one solitary field in France, Tuscany loses out.
The French wheat grows in soil with just the right
combination of minerals and worms, and is *nonpareil*.
The best baker in Paris choses only it for his bread,
baking the most delicious baguettes in the world.
C'est vrai! His *boulangerie* sells out early, baguettes
for all, all until the last generation, usually the oldest,
has left the shop and swallowed their last luscious bite.–

Fallen leaves in the cemetery cover grave markers' names.
Is all of life recognition? Well, I uncover these unknown,
the gone. With my cane's tip I whoosh their names back
into daylight. The Erikas and Jozefs, the Francoises
and Jeans, the Billies and the Bo's. Welcome back again!

About the Very Few Sightings of Jaguars in the Wild ...

    for Jan Hoffman Colston

... also Delilah died. Delilah the West River rancher.
End then of small impromptu parties. Her dark eyes
keen as a surgeon's under the operating table's lamp.

... also the country church. Just a shell of the old now.
The good wood floors, stripped; the pews sold. Organ gone.
Jangling, the piano shoved down into the basement.

And the congregation's women, forgotten. Their
Saturday spring cleaning splurges, their squadron
of milk cans full of water since the church had none.

Someone needs to come along with a can of gasoline
someone said, light a match and put it out of its distress.
They shoot old horses, don't they?

It wasn't good enough to be listed on the National Registry.

... and we will be in awe of their bones and fossils.
And human hawks will feed where grasses once parted
for the slink of a jaguar, her amber eye.

Different Arrangements

1982

" ... *for her distress had allowed no arrangement;*"

Jane Austen, Mansfield Park

Old Lines

Still in the bird lie all the lines
to snake. The tail shorter, the fangs
sharpen to beak. In the same way
their small heads cock, their bodies start
at the noise of a leaf.

The same onyx eyes in the snake
I see in the sparrow perched on a rail
in the sun. Feathers and random streaks
congeal to scaled skin with stripes flowing
evenly, classically down the clean back

into the belly and rising in patterns
as highly structured as Alhambra's mosaics.
Picture a snake there.
It writhes its "s" across the patterned tiles,
sensing ahead on the mosque's porch

near an arch a great deluge of sun.
Hard to decide which pattern—
the tiles' or the scales' or the snake's—
offers the most careful surprise.
Ancient snake. Ancient struggle,

when the ancestor still lives.
It strips down to a raw hunger
for each other, the bird's talons
drip with dead snake, or the snake forces
slowly down its long, tube neck, the bird.

Low warning rattles, quick snaps in the grass.
Nervous rhythms of ingestion. Then come
the liquid movements, the bird's song,
and from the snake's dark dwelling
its practiced silence, perfect sound.

Near the Iris

Imagine you're the five-year-old,
standing beside the bed of iris,
dressed in your mom's old raincoat.
From inside the house
comes the sound of a piano
gone wild; your father
pounding away on your mother,
a sound punctuated by soft
protestations, an occasional
scream after the thud of a
perfectly-placed hit.

This sound you know is all
out of musical balance.
You concentrate on the beautiful
fists of the iris,
their softness.

You try to stay away
from the edge of your stomach.
Which way to go?

This is a problem a lost
 love-ring must have. The sound
you hear keeps looking for it—
the wrong place fingered
over and over.

It's here,
near the iris,
misplaced in your mom's raincoat
pocket. It's there,
in the house, inside father's infallible fist.

Night Out with Mom

Before you unlock the door
you pause to consider
what you could send
back with me tomorrow:
one thing more,
a jar of cherries?
You look from me to the face
of the brightest star in the sky,
"That's Mama," you confide.

Star, star, grandmother star!
Home of my mother's daydreams,
cherries in the rented farmhouse,
named star in a cluster
of seven at the table,
all made of Mama's own stuff,
cold light and dust.

With all Grandmother's might
I command myself to you.
My arms move

but you've opened the door.
We enter single file,
mother, daughter. Grandmother
shines on
an arm's length
above the roof.

IN CONVERSATION WITH GERTRUDE STEIN

What I read into the sentence
is my fantasy:
I'm watching Alice B. Toklas
serve *Eiskaffee* for tea.

She holds the tray
for Gertrude Stein,
Fernande Olivier,
and last, for me.

Fernande's titters
as she glances at my ankles
close together make me wonder
who she is.

Gertrude Stein intercepts
the thought, explains
how Fernande is close
to Picasso and moves on
to talk of cars. Fords.

Don't ever, she advises,
learn reverse.
Just get the stick
out of diddle and dawdle
and slip into third.

I don't like the lurch,
says Alice as Fernande
licks whipped cream
from the corners of her lips.

I take another cookie –
they're superb, but crumbly.
I brush off my chest. Crumbs
fly all over the page.

Alice fades looking spotty.
I have to leave, a little early.
And the other two agree,
yes, I really must go home.
.

At the Banquet to Honor Rousseau

Apollinaire was to be there!
And I wanted badly to be there and
I came, too, on Gertrude Stein's
long sentences and sat near the door
though not so far back as some poor
woman who waited all night alone
in the courtyard for her man.
Fernande fixed the *ríz* and Salmon
(who obviously had a drinking problem)
jigged on top the saw-horse tables.
When he ate the brilliant yellow *fantaisie*
off Alice's new black velvet hat
Gertrude Stein came over,
asked me where I was from in Dakota.
"Near the Standing Rock Sioux Reservation."

Suddenly the center moved toward me.
Apollinaire asked me to sing 'red airs.'
My fingers drumming on the planks, I
droned what I'd heard in the westerns
and they liked it and
Miss Stein was glad I had something
americaine to offer and
if they all saw through it,
so? It was fun! It was *rigolo*.
Then Apollinaire jumped up to sing his poem.
We all sang response,
"*La peinture de ce Rousseau*,"
and it was great and I felt French,
Gertrude Stein, and thanks
for letting me come in on your long sentences.

The Poet's Double

The telephone rings—it's for the poet.
Who's this? I ask. *The New Yorker?*
You want her latest poem? She's flown
the coop. To escape the list, she said.
Today, shopping: groceries and liquid
plumber. We pour the plumber down,
let it settle as we make supper,
put away groceries, feed the cat and
change the bedding. By that time,
we'll have eaten, the drain will be
unclogged so we can do the washing. What?
Yes, it's a round-the-clock life.
I keep order so she can write.
Lightning struck this morning.
She said I've got a paycheck for a heart,
a wad of guilt in my frontal lobe,
an obsession somewhere between
Teresa of Avila's and Cinderella's.
What we need, she shouted, is more
Virginia Woolf. Who? I asked,
and she burst into tears,
wasting more of her writing time.
I mean, if she really wanted to,
she'd just sit down and get at it.
(After we finish the taxes, that is.
We'll get a refund. We want the money.)
You say you pay for poems?
I'm sorry she missed your call.
She mumbled something about warmer parts
as she stumbled out the door
which she didn't bother to close,
wasting fuel. Well, we'll pay for it,
I make sure, one of us always does.

Snake

Poor snake, never to fly
from the underside of leaves
or the warm spot on the rock as
cocoons can when transformed.

Instead you writhe
across the sand on your belly,
the support of your brain and
the length of your tail.

Dark monk! You delight
in keeping your head
properly in place
under your hood.

With no arms or hands
you slough off your skin.
You scare us, we make you
a symbol of life.

But I Won't Go Out in a Boat

1991

"The fulcrum of America is the Plains, half sea half land."

Charles Olson

Do Not Disturb

Do not disturb the sea in this house.
Do not make waves by leaping to fear.
Even a wake like a muskrat's through reeds
upsets the house Neptune, the angry face
behind trident and storm.

Do not think less of yourself, caged,
longing like the shipwrecked for a shore.
Even boats fail here, their hulks
quaver underwater among wrecks
of armchairs, tables, beds, shadowed

stumps in channels of light.

Like a Church

Like a church on the North Sea,
the Berlin Baptist
stands on a hilltop, a spare,
big-boned house looking over
a sea of marsh and fields.

The walls run a good
fist thick
against the tides
of wind.
Two bars,
gun-barrel thin,
prop up the window frame.

Mullions square off the glass.
In the theology of rods they come
from four directions at once
to tame, bind, and confound
the scope of the vision as well as to divide
the immensity of the Great
Plains into parcels—

each pane, a handspan
wide. What light
falls in, remains,
the messenger from heaven,
underfoot among fixed benches.

On Sunday my grandfather comes to sing.
Pumped music rolls just over the tops of high notes.
His voice rolls like a breaker just under the crest,
all the way down to the end of a song and will not be rushed.

In the pause between hymns
you can hear the wind,
the sound of the farm,
the people I come from.
And its taste on the tongue is grit.

Homecoming

At midnight the man comes home from his shift.
He pulls a chair up to his daughter's bed.
"Where's your mother?" The girl pretends
to sleep. Her braids sprawl across the pillow.
She is very near, behind the Hollywood headboard,
in the V-space in the corner where she's slept
close to the girl for a week now. He asks again,
not nice anymore. "Where is she?" Slowly
she crawls out. The girl braces for her mother's
next beating, but he pushes the chair back instead.
He glares at his wife. He goes in to their bed.
She follows in the still night. In the morning
they sit at their regular places around the table.

Taking a Snow Bath

It's simple when there's powder snow.
You find a barren space—a field of silence
between parents. You put on a cloak,
the color and sweep of blue jay wings
and then, so no one can see where it is
you're coming from, you sweep down—
cloak-tail, wing-sleeves gloriously
flying—Whoosh! You're in diamond snow.
You come up in whatever character you want.
I choose Bird, bachelor aunt. She ruffles
her feathers, sputters at a bath
when the kitchen's cold. With a long
blue shiver, she works the snow down
through oil and the dirt in her wings,
taking every grain she needs to come clean.
Then she flits her head and is gone.
The prints left behind are small,
but the wing marks, precise as knife cuts,
and the bad blood, pure.

Playing His Heart Out

for my North German uncles

That day we were trapped
between chartreuse living
room walls and the godly
cleanliness of afghans
saving sofa and chairs.

We were talking about
anything except Uncle Carl–
gone, how we'd miss him–
when Uncle Gus came down
the hall and stood in

the archway, his wiry
body strapped under a black
accordion. "Haven't played,"
he said, "for a long time."
So he played a waltz and I

squirmed in my chair under
the slow flow of grief. He
played a polka and I heard
my sister clapping lightly
for the mourner, his head held

over the keys, his cheekbones
red and high as Helgoland's
cliffs on the North Sea. Gulls
whirled and screamed around
the black load on his heart.

Rabbit

I went out of my house
to look at the moon.
Moon, hidden by trees.
But under the trees
in shadow, in grass,
I saw a small rabbit
like Dürer's, the same
throb in its throat.

During the Blizzard

Under the wagon bed
sits a young woman,
my grandmother-to-be,
spending the winter.
Cowchip and sod walls
keep out the full
blast of north wind.

And tonight
as a mean band of snow
hurls itself
against my city's walls,
the shadow of her small
room darkens
the fruit on my table.

They Come Humming

What is the keyboard
but a variation on a table,
a trough in ivory and ebony
for all the Hungry
to come to and be
soothed by food's music–

>his head is bowed.
>Like the pianist at an old Knabe,
>Grandfather Gottlieb at the table
>flexes his thick speckled fingers
>over the plate and beings to hum
>for the 15,633rd time,
>*Komm Herr Jesu, sei unser Gast*
>*und segne was Du uns bescheret hast.*
>Amen. Then he lifts
>fork and knife to the sausage and
>snaps the fried skin.

Eating is a reminder of
your link in the Great Chain of Being,
though Grandfather, *der Gottlieb*,
never knew life by that name.

>I do and I sit alone.
>Remembering the power
>in rings and chains,
>I set no place at my table
>for old names, but still
>they come, down aisles
>in waist-high wheat fields
>towards my table, single file,
>out of groves of ashes,
>black-scarfed, with a ring
>in one ear, big-bellied
>Germans from Russia,
>they come humming.

Stranger in Her House

1995

"My father? Had a sweetheart in Mom's house?
Another stranger in her house I never met."

On My Mother's Death: Harvesting

In this north where combines cut
swaths through the wheat's blond walls, she
stares out the station window, looking for clouds
of dark smoke and the train wheels' rumbling.

She will not be afraid to start anew,
to leave a gray-roofed house, the one
where she lived. The one where we live.

When the iron horse shakes the platform
she'll board, saying, "What a lovely
thing to find." And I'll wave goodbye.
What a lovely thing to lose.

In His Hands

On the evening of my mother's funeral I come home to my dad.
It is as if what I've always feared has happened: He has
    killed her.
Now the dread springs to life: I'll be forced to sit alone here
    with him, too.
And he will be very nice to me, how he couldn't be with her.

And that is how it is. From the front door I see him through
    the screen.
He's sitting in his chair. His shirt's off. He wears a strapped
    undershirt,
suspenders, black trousers, and slippers run down in the heel,
    the way
I wear shoes down. Over the arms of the chair his huge hands
    rest,
brown crushers and hammerers, they hang from their thick
    wrists. Quietly
dangle. Hands undone, without purpose, with her gone.

Reins

In the kitchen,
that small space
between porch door and oven,
my mother stood behind me
and braided my hair,
a sun-bleached mane in her hands.

Three strands she wove
over and under, a design
twisting the future
with the lost, her past,
until two long ropes
hung down my back.

On this dreamy morning,
long after her funeral,
my mother tugs, left
and right on my head,
in no hurry, she nor I,
to let go.

The Other Mozart

2001

"... dearest Sister ... Please trust me absolutely and never think that I shall forget you; but remember that things do not always turn out, or at least not always exactly, as one wishes."

    Wolfgang Mozart

All I Want

The way the wolf walks
even within the walls of the city
it's a wonder
as many people live as do.

Money, Nannerl, money is the reason, Papa says.

Moneymoneymoney, the Wunderkinder sing to the king.
Moneymoneymoney, the ironmonger sings to the banker,
the butcher to the brewer, the baker to the joiner.
Wolf is hungry, Money,
Wolfgang, money is the reason
to make music, Papa says.

Years of bread and potato
turn the sisters' faces yellow.
Wolf slathers close to the convent,
swallows a peasant in the field instead.
Behind fortress walls the Archbishop eats
all the dumplings his mother sets
before him.

Moneymoneymoney, the wolf sings
over the common grave, over the sarcophagus,
looking for a market.
"All I want
is to make music and be rich."

>	the sound of
>	one student
>
>	counting
>	out two
>
>	*kreuzer*
>	for the lesson and
>
>	the plink
>	gyring on the music stand.

Between Art and Usefulness

Listen how the iron comes sighing to the clavier:
See how much useful, simple work I've gotten done!
Three of Papa's shirts, his jacket, Nannerl's dress,
white tablecloth, hall curtains, towels, sheets,
the household underpinnings pressed
flat and smooth, white as drone.
And what can you say you've done, Clavier,
standing in your anonymity of uselessness?
How have you pushed the stone?
how have you made it move along
as it does, slug, slug, slug?

Nannerl Mozart: Speaking of Her Retirement

"We are as fit as one can be in this dull Salzburg."
　　—Nannerl Mozart, twenty years old

Home. Woman with cat, canary and Bimperl the dog.
With mother and clavier and a shared room:
one of Papa's students sleeps on the red couch
at my bedroom door. I go for long walks.
Merchants smile in passing. They think they have
what I want and there's money for it in my pocket.
—What, Sirs, is the cost of praise?
The devil himself offers an idea.
I send it to Wolferl under my name.
He writes back, "I'm amazed
to find how well you can compose.
In a word, the song is beautiful."
—What is the cost, Sirs, of praise?
The brittle scratch of pen on paper?
A song that dies without a singer?

Nannerl Mozart: Fashioning a Single Response

"*I hope my queen, that you are enjoying ... health and that now and then ... you will sacrifice for my benefit some of your important and intimate thoughts ...*"

—Wolfgang Mozart to Nannerl, Vienna, August 14, 1773

I hope my sensitive ass, that you receive my sacrifice
pawing, pouncing, snorting and horsing around in courts
and/or any other low place where His Highness allows
idle tongues to wag begging for thought—yours,
like any ass's, comes at the end where an asinine
demand traditionally & charitably exists
though marginally on a page; namely, in the P.S.,
a flatulent last blast which you, dear Arse,
were so wont to deliver in the practice room—
crepidos ventris which resembled the squall
from a brass section squatting on a hill
of Bavarian dung. My dear little Beetlebomb,
even the stoutest nose (how related the word
nose is to noise!) would have flinched, as do
equine-nostriled Viennese when they possess
during feverish *Sommerhitze* an especially keen sense
of smell and source, and where a prodigious horn
like yours is small advantage—I digress, however,
from fulfilling your request. Enclosed lie two intimate
thoughts for my donkey monkey, the little A-hole
in a cherry red suit, the great *Wunder Arse* at the keyboard,
der Herr Dr. Wiggly Butt in the parlor but not the boudoir
(or? yet?), the twin to my own brown braying heart. No. 1:
Shit in your bed and make a good mess. No. 2: Remember
the sad smell of your own sweet queen Lick My Arse.

Nannerl Mozart on Names: Trazom

"I do hope that Wolfgang will make his fortune in Paris quickly …."
　　　　　　　　—Mamma Mozart, 1777

God's will. God's time. A long time
before fame and fortune, Wolfgang.
Maybe Big Money comes slowly
because you're always riding away
from us, off to Munich, to Paris,
to lunch at Count Blah's house.
And when you use an alias—Gnagflow
Trazom—God can't find you.

If only we knew which language He loves best!
Wolfgang, when you pray beside your bed
say your name clearly. Remind God
in French—Amadé, in Latin—Amadeus,
in Greek—Theophilus, in Italian—Amedeo,
in German—Gottlieb, that he, above all, loves you.

Leopold Mozart: On the Cross

Don't alibi for him, Nannerl. It isn't the Archbishop
Wolfgang wants to be rid of, it's me, his own father, his teacher,
his one true friend. The old man is useless, throw
his work and suffering and sacrifice to the wind.

God only knows how Wolfgang will pay
for nailing me to this cross. But he will. Debts of
honor and duty; over one thousand gulden
squandered while your dear mother was alive.

God forgive us all she died, chaperoning him,
alone, sick, in a stinking Parisian hotel room,
bled insufficiently, on a fast day. And Wolfgang
pays the bleeder for it *after* she's died!

In the very next letter he's mentioning that
slut Aloisia Weber. He will "make her career."
Make her career! The puffed-up *Gogelkopf*.
The meathead! I tell you, I get so angry ...

chi va piano, va sano, I tell him. Who goes softly
goes sanely. But not Wolfgang. No.–Luck
is with him. In Vienna he will make us at least
a thousand a year. Ha! A thousand promises.

He's sending me a stick, Nannerl, a walking stick
that I should "use instead of him and always
carry it." I could break it. I could break the back
of his house with it had he not already broken

mine. Oh, Nannerl, he will eat his words.
And we, hapless, misguided mice shall starve
with him under the eye of the Arch Lummox,
long-toothed, laughing on his Mönchsberg throne.

"Improvisator!" The bishop called me once.
The name rolled down to my feet.
Yes. I improvise a rock to build my house
upon, and it turns into a walking stick.

Pros & Cons: A Marriage of Convenience

—Nannerl Mozart's to the Prefect, Johann Baptist von Berchtold zu Sonnenburg, Freiherr/Baron

If only he were English!
(She loves the English.)
If only he had come

from
anywhere else
but St. Gilgen

flashing his title, his house, his stability. His money
sucking up her bankruptcy, her virginity, the shreds
of her former glory

and guaranteeing her
four hours daily practice.
Papa approves. And pushes.

And she? Well, she's
thirty-three; he's forty-eight;
he may die first.

Winter of 1784-85

Cattle stand hungry in the snow,
their ribs like pitchfork tines.
The *Wienerblättchen* reports the road
to Linz is blocked. As is St. Gilgen's.

In every corner stands the iron
rod of cold. In the yard dogs
scavenge in a pile of trash—frozen
fish guts and menstrual rags.

Beams insure the house
won't cave in under the weight
of a second story and the eight
stairways, the narrowest, a chute

to the kitchen, to stove and churn Cook
hides behind. "Anything wrong, Mum?"
—In the hall opposite Mamma's portrait
Kaiser Joseph II frowns down.

The *Kachelofen* warms the parlor
and *Ofensitzer*—children and their father.
Six tin-eared Gilgeners on the bench.
Warders of one pregnant Salzburger.

THE GLASS LADY

Glassware and bottles. That's what I hauls.
And personal delivery service if you miss the postal coach.
Regular: Once a week between St. Gilgen and Salzburg.
That's how I met the Mozarts. The Mister in Salzburg,
the Daughter in St. Gilgen. Ja, and if I had just one kreuzer
for every time I've driven the wagon up to Number 8
—the old Tanzmeister's house in the Hannibalplatz—
and the package for the Daughter wasn't ready.
"A minute, a minute!" he snipes. I glares. Why not?
As if it's my fault he's late!
Herr Fuss and Clamor storms about the room.
Herr Bustle von String and Scissor.
Such an old man. "Take your time," I tells him.
"It's your money lost, if something gets broken."
He cinches his bundles with double knots.
I gives the old codger my highest praise,
"You would've made a good shipper."

Everything from duck to broken clavichord string
the Daughter sends him. "Don't lose it," she says, pulling
on my sleeve. I hates it when they pulls on my sleeves.
"I never lose wares," I mutters. "Not if they're packaged good."
And would I want to steal her fishy-smelling clavichord string?
She thinks I'm running short?
"No, Mum," I says, bunching her packages down good
between bottles and straw in the wagon bed.
"It's important," she says. —What they all say.—
"It's the lake," she says. "Strings snap. Then I can't play."
Oh, I knows what snaps in the Prefect's house. Cook tells me.
It's in the marriage contract, don't you know: Four hours a day
the wife plays, the five kids go wild in the house.
Their racket floats out the windows with her music and the Prefect's
voice, tighter than a knot: "Someone keep them QUIET!"
Cook says she's played for the King of England Himself.
She gets no raves from me; if I don't haul, she don't play.

A Blue Note

The success of other women musicians:
Regina Strinasacchi, Nancy Storace. The established
Josepha von Auernhammer, Maria Theresia von Paradis,
Madame Bitzenberg, the damned Davies sisters.
Even Constanza Weber, that two-bit squeaking
field mouse, procured a solo at St. Peter's.
Only because of Wolfgang! The list lengthens,
a struggle against envy. Therese Friberth.
Gretl Marchand, her latest three sonatas.
Carnival has been a fairyland of awards for her –
a shower of earrings, pendants, pearls, bracelets–
Count von Seeau's gifts to the brilliant sixteen-year-old
who is so at home with the new pianoforte.
"You'd like the touch, Nannerl," she writes,
it's so easy to play. I could show you how in a minute."

Playing Four Hands with Wolfgang

—In Memoriam: Nannerl Mozart on her brother's death

Wolferl, Wolferl,
what are we going to do with you!

                They forgot, the rats! She
                got sick. The coach was

What have we done to you?
What will happen to you—so
sweet, so ravenous?

                late. The Count implored
                and I had to stay. The King

You will eat us alive.
We will eat you alive.

                of Prussia himself was
                there and demanded it of
                 me. The

Have eaten you alive.

                weather was foul, the
                wheel fell off. We couldn't

Boy wonder, stuck in the elephant's
basket and paraded under a canopy

                get horses. The time was
                not ripe. The prima donna

in the land of flesh-eating
pygmies. *Wunder* sized-up
as a one-swallow meal

                failed miserably, the old
                cow. The inn was too

Wolferl, sweet Jack Pudding,
Sultan of the Kingdom of Rücken,

                                        expensive but the town
                                        was full, what else, Nannerl,

my little brother, my partner, my Wolferl,
my villain, my rascal, my Wolfgang Amadé!

                                        could I have done?

The Visit

> The English couple, Vincent and Mary Novello, visit
> bedridden Nannerl Mozart, July 15, 1829.

they will not forget
(they wrote it in their journals)
how they brought her a birthday gift
a fortnight early (flowers? wine?),
how pleased the old woman was,
the broken shape, once the little girl
in the painting above her bed

they will remember her
efforts to speak, out
of excitement to show them
the excellent instrument–
"Yes, yes, you may play it!"–
although she no longer could play, not even
a favorite, Wolfgang's "*O cara armonia*"

(she had wanted to practice
for *die Engländer*, for their visit;
her nephew, Wolfgang's son,
offered to carry her in his arms
to the cembalo but the voyage was
too long for her; mid-room, he'd had
to return the nightshift of bones)

back in London, the Novellos
will listen to the Requiem
in the Portuguese Embassy chapel
they will remember her
hands, how like theirs
they'd wanted to touch again
what Wolfgang had

The Rhubarb King

2006

"Nobody remembers their names today,
And yet their hands were real once ..."

– Czesław Miłosz

The Rhubarb King

The rhubarb king sits in the garden,
resting under the arms of a hackthorn,

that ancient tree, while the court photographer–
my sister, his daughter–snaps him there.

His curved-handled cane leans
like a good dog against his leg.

His cap is slanted, his cheeks shaved,
his mustache–once fine and black, sleek

and mean has turned into an old king's
cowcatcher. His eyes guarded, defying,

run to blue, as if his kingdom was not
always as bountiful or beautiful as wanted,

not as smashing as the rhubarb stalks
he grips, like nightsticks, giant, leaf-topped

scepters on his left and right, clubs
that furl into heart-shapes, toxic, oil-tough

with ruffled edges. Like the kingdom
I ran from.

In the window behind this instant,
among sun catchers and a row of snake plants

withering in crockery, I see the ethereal
form in the palace, the rhubarb queen.

I can make out a wing, her chest,
her garlanded head. She's

peering past the king as if calling,
calling for her hands. His are there, brown

and strong. How is she to make something
sweet of his kingdom, without hands?

And hers were dear, very dear and deft.
—My sister, long after the king's death,

sends me this photo. I take it upon myself
to write the caption: All history is myth.

Washing My Face

This morning when I cupped my hands to rinse my face,
when I lifted them, eyes closed,
the image they carried
up out of nowhere, out of the water, after all these years,
that same old thing, my father, bent over,
beating my mother; her twisted face. Bent over
the sink, hands dripping, I waited
for the scene to pass, all the while shaking.
That this can keep coming up.
That this can keep coming up.
That my own hands keep bringing it up
out of the well.

FROM "ROOMS"

Moon

Moon comes early to the bedroom, to the mirror
of the man with the heavy-lidded eye. His bed doubles
in the reflection, glass filming, milking what will happen:
Moon crawling on her belly, all the way across the earth,
to offer him her robe and bathe his feet in light.

Windows

His are old, puffy as eyelids, the paint peels
like dried sleep, windows in need of washing.
They're fine if you don't touch them. But tap
with a hammer–top left, bottom right–to straighten
the warp, and you'd make it worse. You might even
smash the glass. Then what would you do, your dad
and you, with so much light inside the house?

Bedroom

The house is arty, the lawn's a picnic, little round tables
and strolling guests. If my dad's out driving his 88 Olds,
he'll run right into this, smudged glasses and all. Where is he
anyway? I peek upstairs in the bedroom–find him asleep
among the coats, his body a spoon to loneliness. Armless
pillow for her dead body. My mother's wig, for her head.

Floors

Mine are glass. If you lift the rug's edge, you can see
down through all the stories. How can glass floors be safe?
These barely, barely hold me. Other renters skim over
their glass floors. They're rich, slim, young as Dad's undertaker,
everything pinned and buttoned down. They party. They sing,
"No problem!" Didn't they see my dad fall? Didn't they see
how his arms flew up–toward me–in surrender?

Zinnia

So much room here on the north side, but shade makes
such a miserable garden, so skimpy, a zinnia just ups and
walks away. Where is the one who can help, who listens
to a garden, as you might listen to a heartbeat?
Parched gumbo skin; the face, a house of north and south
passages; ears, like yours and mine, caves; eyes, grottos.
In the recesses, a blue mirage of light.

Remembering the Acts
Done to the Dead

behind the cop on the motorcycle,
behind the little orange fender flags fluttering

at the church basement's paper-covered tables
in rows that rasp with the weight

of what's coming to us
in the Ladies Aide Circle's lunch

of judgment-green jello,
of white, bought-bread sympathy

in lumps, hard
to swallow.

In a Russian Garden
after Matthew 7: 9-11

This evening I saw my father
on a bench in the garden's shade.
I saw him easily from the gate.
I said to myself, I'll draw him out.
Father, I called from the gate,
give me a fish, I am hungry.
And I held out my bag for a scorpion.
Father, I called again from the gate,
give me bread for my journey.
And I held out my bag for a stone.
I called, Father, kiss me
and I held my hanky ready
to wipe the spittle off my cheek.
Slowly he rose from the bench.
He took my bag and filled it
from the evening's dark rows.
He hugged me once,
over the gate between us,
and gave back the sack.
It bulged with proof.
I hurried to my friend's house,
dumped the bag on her table–
out rolled cabbages, cucumbers, tomatoes.
My friend's eyes rolled up to heaven.
She didn't believe.
Lies! Lies! I cried. Again
he hasn't given me what I need!
No stones! No scorpions.

Duet in the Little Blue Church

Listening to him
you'd think we two sang
the way the saved sing,
making the connection
between loss and love,
holding its music,
cracking stars,
my dad's bass to my alto.

Listening to him,
you'd think sorrow
our beacon,
joy, the rose
light over snow.

You'd even think
disappointment–
sitting in the back pew,
unfrozen from frowning–
had opened its mouth, as echo.

Hands

We have identical hands, my father and I.
Extra large, hard to find gloves for.
My father folds his out of habit
when the Preacher prays.

A mass on his belly.
A belief in the Testaments' yoke,
a scripture of rest and work.
Unfolded they return to chores.

Incredible inventions they are.
Our constant song, that anyone
should have been so smart
to have thought of making hands!

Must have been a German.
Like peasants we tend ours, oiling
and binding the bruises with a barn-like
collection of funnels and rags.

We'll never throw our hands away.
When we visit, we keep them in boxes,
avoiding accidental touch, but look:
Yours. Mine. Worlds. Within reach.

In His Car

My father's driving down 83, from North
to South Dakota. "Full moon out,"
he tells me later on the phone.
"Big as he can be. No wind.
No cars on the road. Just go, go."

On the road under the moon
my father has not yet met his conqueror,
some superior death machine,
motionless and moonless. He drives
undefeated in his kingdom, which I can find

listed only in my records.

THE OLD MAN MAKES IT

From his doorstep he can see a path
where snowdrifts are less deep, like
a trail along the slope of a mountain,
where, if you rely on poles and go slow,
you could climb it.
The old man vows he'll do it.
The old man with gray stubble on his chin.

Once he skirts the whale of a ridge,
the body that tails right up
to his house, then curls like a wave
or snarled lip, the rest will be easy.
With broom sticks, held broomhead up,
he'll scale it, with two old brooms,
planted like poles in the snow.

He can feel the wind raw
on the back of his legs,
as if he wore straw.
Up slope, down slope, without
friendly back-up, across a world's
glacier to the garden shed, his base camp.
His breath huffs. His thumping heart cheers.

Watching Two Crows Circle

Hunger is strong and curious. Defiant, won't move.
It is snow midway up the cornstalk.
It is morning. It is frost on a field of thistle.
Morning frost across a field of weeds.
It is a black peck in the snow with no kernel of corn
forthcoming.
It is the field oak's bare height.
It is a field the deer have gleaned.
A crazy shag of black wings through weeds,
a shunt through watery hoarfrost.
It is the screaming and warning I.
It is for corn, through corn, in corn.
It is stomach. It is one seeking trinity.

Calling

2010

"… those maddening little women who kept calling, calling to each other …"
        Elizabeth Bishop

Portraits of Sister Maria Celeste, Daughter to Galileo Galilei, a Poem in Fourteen Sayings

1. Money Solves Most Problems

                        If one has it,
one can buy any sacrifice on earth.
Galileo's daughters, dropped off
at the convent's gate, are ushered in
by a moneyed palm. It buys their future.
And pomegranate and aloe, bread
when the two will starve, a pad for
cold stomachs when the abbess,
la Madonna, determines the blankets
must be gathered for storage, despite
a freakish return to cold weather.

                        Only innocents
think confinement and a name change–
from Virginia to Suor Maria Celeste, from
Livia to Suor Arcangela–come for free.

2. The Heavenly Father Sends Our Earthly Father to Love Us

At last Suor Celeste has a cell to herself.
No more nights sleeping with four sisters.

Sire, her father, unearths some money to buy quiet.
She had only the pittance she receives as pay.

How she regrets the seven hours sleep
her body demands. In that luxury, dreams

and oblivion, the sisters of San Matteo
rarely drift. Lord knows how

their poverty enlightens the world.
Villagers believe the sisters' prayers

are especially heard. Seeing the state
of her heart, Suor Celeste prays for sugar

to sweeten its sender to its receiver
in this otherwise miserable world.

3. Earth Offers Us a Taste of Heaven

I live in this miserable world of lovely places.
Fading sunlight from the convent's orchard
streams through the refectory window at dusk,
ambering the bleached table top and oak chairs.
On autumn mornings under a lavender sky
the peasants' lane leads to an orange-veiled
meadow and fields bordered by cypress.
The path sinks softly with dew underfoot.
In the chapel I love the tabernacle door's
click. I caress Holy Mary's arm, smooth
travertine. Oh. No colder than mine.

4. It Is No Wonder the Poor Are Poor in Spirit

Galileo's little mule,
a beast of burden,

hired out and badly mistreated,
a sweet, faithful, four-legged menial

led by Geppo, makes a six-legged duo,
born to convey parcels and letters

to and from Galileo's daughter.
Homesick for its master,

confused by human borders,
the ass brays its strange song,

defenseless and invisible, known
by the martyred, other world.

5. The Seasons Go Round in Order

The citron sweetening in its season
she candies for her father. The rule
she follows turns from wine to vinegar.

She turns the cloth that makes the collar,
makes soap for a collar's washing.
The tears—gaps as raggedly loose

in the world as her Sire's ideas
in court—she mends. As if the sun
could circle the earth. There!

—A knot is made; thread, snapped.
The threads, moved as in a fugue.
The fact is stitched: This planet

Earth revolves around the sun!
Sun would never bow to earth. Proof
is right under everyone's pointed nose.

See?—The dark-robed planets in Rome,
orbiting around il *Papa*'s throne,
genuflect and kiss his golden ring.

6. The Necessity for Wine Can't Be Ignored

Suor Celeste sips it, training her tongue—
with its thirteen-year-old taste for loving
sweet, abhorring sour—not to cringe.

Unlike her sister Suor Arcangela who
favors the good red wine Sire sends.
Who can trust the water in Tuscany?

During prayer, one doesn't meditate
on Jesus; the water, the blood
can be fraught with disease.

Wine, too, carries its own
chancy cravings. No safety
can be imbibed in this world.

But what is Galileo's daughter doing?
She who should be so busy mending
that I–she–cannot think.

7. The Heart Is Often Embattled

To fear the Heavenly Father and His rod.
   To love the earthly father and his face.

To pray to Him always, hourly.
   Mindful of his absence, to correspond daily.

As late as the third hour of the evening
   the wise heart-beat, the watch, the minute

ask blessings from the disciplines He sends.
   To know him in your heart and mind and feet,

the path dust knows. In the cask's fermentation
   to recognize the Lord is close.

   To adore the path he treads to visit you.

To remember Him always in everything you do.
   To care that he not get sick. To care that he is old.

(In the apothecary, to prepare pills for his maladies,
saffron for his stomach. Papal pills for headache.)

To know everything comes from Him. To know
  blood drums love for him each moment.

  To thank him for making you in love. (How
  could he leave you then?)

To thank Him for this convent.

8. Good Wine: It Is But One Remedy for Good Health

The best remedy during pestilence is distance.
The outer door kept latched. The peep-hole shut.
If she boils the mutton to string, Suor Celeste can get it down.
If she works extra hard, though feeble, she can do the chores
of the nun who lies in bed, ill, unable to raise her head.
If she keeps an eye on the level of wine in the casks,
there's enough at the table to go 'round all winter.
Can the Lord make out the herbalist's small figure
in the garden?–Of the convent's flasks, viols, amphora,
she knows. Of herbs and citrons and syrups.
Of poultices and ointments, recipes passed along
by word of mouth. Isn't there always hope?
What evil tongue would speak malice? For what purpose?
That the sick should suffer, that there is no hope?

9. Lifting Up Your Heart Is Beneficial: Antiphon

As in directing the choir. One of Suor Celeste's chores.
    One that's not paid enough, monthly or daily.
As in singing the music for the Eucharist, Christ's high drama.
    One re-enacted at Mass for our benefit.
As in a holy day, not to be profaned by a priest.

        One unfit to bless the sacraments.
As in a man who's bought the sacred position.
        One with free wine and free pinching.
As in a steady supply because nuns can't run away.
        One terrible, shameful muddle.
As in writing to Galileo, to petition at least the bishop.
        One real priest: Could His Excellency find one for us?
As in a priest who can celebrate the Eucharist.
        One not needing Suor Celeste's prompting.
As in receiving for one's sacrifice more than a jot and tittle.
As in wearing new linen wimples.
        Oh! One looks thus donned quite beautiful.

10. Love Is the Best War; Arm Yourself with Weapons

Celeste:	Sire likes my nutmeg stomach balm.
Arcangela:	But my rosemary flower jam better!
Both:	Our elixirs. Our roses of sugar for Sire,
Celeste:	our father, who lets not one star go by
Arcangela:	without a letter, sending his best
Celeste	wines and wishes, a *moggio* of wheat,
Arcangela:	and a pair of worn collars
Both:	which we bleach and return.
	We are so entirely in love with him.
Celeste:	Even the charming, yellow kitten
Arcangela:	who found, in the courtyard,
Celeste:	the basket of thrushes Sire sent,
Arcangela:	and ate the top two,
Celeste:	receives our forgiveness.
Both:	Who knows?
Arcangela:	Perhaps *la gattina* liberated the birds
Celeste:	out of the goodness in her heart.

11. One Sickens of Sickness

Today slowed me down considerably.
My tasks ambled on ahead of me, and I
never really caught up on the path.

Thanks to my pills, and a flask
of Sire's good wine, la Madonna
lies quiet in bed at this time,

after stabbing herself with a knife,
and striking her head against the floor.
We fear her and for her.

I pray for our bad deeds
and secret vices. What evil
could the Holy Mother not dispel

by Her presence? May the procession
carrying the Merciful Virgin on the road
to Florence, pass this way soon.

12. A Small Garden Has the Large Garden's Troubles

This is my mouth, the one which drinks and speaks.
Small you may notice, a small drawer to a cabinet
which is usually quite empty. Hollow.
Only a few teeth left inside that chamber; no matter,
those that are present, ache. I smile behind my hand
at their bounty in my world of repaired clocks.
Sire's clocks. His skills are superb at repair.
He must not forget me. Oh, not! Then my life,
already so small, just my sister and I, and
the Almighty, a few dried figs, some meatless soup,
would shrink to nil. Sire sends us a pot
of caviar to fill us up. It does not suit me.
My stomach churns at asking for plainer fare,

for I am always demanding of Sire some favor,
more than my share. I pray for sun and rain.
An equal supply of both; thus the garden's
broad beans and our lemons need not struggle.

13. Luck Sometimes Occurs Naturally

Suor Angelica is now draper.
She has lost her position of cellarer,
having enjoyed the wine too much.
She's now in charge of bleach.

Thanks be to God. At his recent death
the farmer adjacent our convent left
his farm to us, guaranteeing eighty
casks of wine this year, *Morselletti*

from God's table, cups of darkness
turned into light. And if, for Advent, Sire
could send from his orchard, a plate of
apricots, our tongues 'd sweeten with joy.

14. Mystery Can Never Be Solved

I dwell in prison; left to my own devices,
I must squirm under the load. Can it possibly be
borne on these shoulders? My body the Small.

A thousand years pass before tomorrow comes,
and yet they go by quickly. Light's eye sees in
to my cell. The universe, Sire writes, is our keep.

And yet, I have these kitchen pleasures, making
sweet comestibles at the stove, breathing in deeply
a fruity wisdom and, like my Sire, giving it all away.

On the Train to Milan, the Conductor, il Controllore

1.
He is not a cheat. Knee to knee in the railroad car,
we balance books on our laps; his, black, mine,
a Berlitz. None of the phrases in it seem to apply;
still, he is kind, too kind, like a father or uncle.
One who knows you cannot set off in a hot, turbulent
world alone without luck as a companion, and that's why,
he sighs, I must pay more. His gestures paw
huge, bosomy surcharges in the air. His face
films with an afternoon of sweat, his voice,
the essence of sadness as he holds out his hand.
Prego, prego. It's a relief, not understanding but
handing over the cash. It could have been so much more;
so many other things gone wrong he could have spotted.
It's enough he's sat down with me, the foreigner.

2.
He's too kind to be a good lover
or cheater. His knee bones pull
on his trouser's twill, creased,
like his face; if he washed it,
he might feel better. He leans
forward, his hands sweating.
What I understand is the sadness
in his outstretched hand.
What I understand is that
essence of happiness in giving
him, of all men, my money.

3.
What is a small price to pay for dear, underpaid tenderness?
Two, three Euros? To have a man on a train sit down
beside you? *Il controllore* is not a cheat. He balances
his intentions with his duties, listed in the black book

on his lap. I pull out my Berlitz. I'm alone, an illiterate
in Italian, already two counts against me. I understand
his brown collie eyes. Prego, Prego. I understand he'll stay
as long as necessary. I understand I'm lucky I can pay.

4.
Poor man. So upset. Trying so hard,
and I don't understand one word
he's saying, sighing, Prego, prego,
poring over his black, opened book.

5.
You must go out expecting to run into
all kinds of weather. You must try to
understand just because you are alone
and can read, somewhat, il controllore's
upset face, his brown, drowning eyes,
the opposite of happiness, his gestures
and words go up in flame whether
the source is understood or not.
For you are in il controllore's section,
and he is nodding over your opened
purse, taking what he wants, and now,
Signora! Triumphant! He'll lead you
over the next hundred kilometers of future.

6.
How is it, a woman will sit alone,
a woman of a certain age, and no one
will see her? She looks out the train window.
Il controllore comes along, he in his once
handsome blue uniform. He with his cap.
His black book and scuffed shoes. He
is the one who sits down beside her. Prego!
He tries to explain in his language,
which she doesn't understand, nor he, hers,
why he sat down. The woman—of great

imagination—smiles at all the reasons
of the heart that could be. None are his.
His, he explains, opening the black book
on his lap, his is a matter of surcharge.
So! There it is, like a pratfall: simply
a matter of money.
                       Which she pays.

The Bürgermeister's Wife's Account

(Salzburg, 1750)

She was sixteen years old when she took to the woods
near her parents' farm, couldn't get along, wouldn't work.
Let her go, I said, she'll tire of stuffing straw in rags for shoes.
Her mother had her carted off to the Rathaus,
had her put in stocks and branded "thief."
The Bürgermeister gave any man on horseback
leave to whip her. Still she thumbed her nose.
Let her eat snow, I said. Who was she after all?
A *Tunichtgut*. Not the kind of woman you'd want
playing clavier while you played violin or brushing
your hair as you watched in the mirror. She was
a liar, lighting fires and showing the between-
her-legs to dogs though she swore she never
swapped the fagot bundle for the dead baby.
No man could have been more filthy-mouthed.
We washed hers out good once, in the Salzach.
And her hole. Dirtier than a pig she was, rutting
in an alley with any man for a crust, both his poker
and her hole greasy as the cobbles they did it on.
Her hair, a vipers' nest. You'd be sitting in the inn,
her face would appear, nose pressed to the window,
a smear of mucus and curse. She was without doubt
hopeless. From her no prince of the Church would
ever collect a single tax. She was easy to push
toward the block; she was as content as the old to go.
When they drew the sword over her head, she laughed.
She was happy when the blade fell. She was.

The Skatplayer's Tale

    for Susanna Margareta Brandt
    b.?, d. 14. Jan. 1772, Frankfurt am Main

A three-liter-wench, in a few more years
she'd 'a been able to schlepp five or six.
"For ye ugly mugs," she'd grunt
and slam the steins down. "For yr
trouble!" we'd yell and feel a little ass under

our boot. Tight ass. Her walk made you
want to get into her pot—why eat soot
instead of porridge?—When the last of us tied
his flap, you could've scraped her off the table.
Hahn said he'd flip her a *kreuzer* at Christmas.

By then the Dreck was over the mountain.
Muck and suck. Even in a cloud of smoke
four smart soldiers could've figured it out,
even that Wurst that calls himself an innkeeper.
The day she told him to blow it out his hole,

her hand shook when she made change,
the smell of afterbirth hung on her
strong as horse. You understand we
regulars, we *Stammtisch*, we would've kept
our mouths shut. But a damned dog

dug up the carcass, dragged it to market,
into the fishwife caw and cackle. The hew
roused black-robed investigators from city hall,
their hems trailed over her room's floor,
got snotted up with bits of bloody brain.

Bashed its head in, she had. Dumb cluck.
She could've drowned it in the Main
with a stone so it wouldn't 'a floated up.
Pure shit between her ears. Wasn't hard
for folks to put two and two together.

God, lawyers, doctors and judge
visited her cell. Even the *Schultheiss*
dropped in to lick ass, and that's as
high an office as you get here in Frankfurt.
All for a whiff of the muck.

So it goes. We sucked tail
and left them the head. And take it
they did. Laid it on the block. Rolled
off easy as a chicken's.–Hey, pot-girl!
Wiggle on over here with another round!

The Last Queen of France

At some point opulence becomes obscene.
The fish on the table, a forkful of flesh,
once delicious, turns into jaded gangrene.

The rest? Amaze me, amaze, amaze.
Think use of alcohol. Weed. Fame. Main
character, the Queen. Taken from mother

tongue, hers is inadequate, no vessel
for the gush, the desired French;
fluency gets stuck in a child's syntax.

A ragged audience waits outside the palace,
ready to stuff its belly at her tables,
and after heaving, purge the Queen's

lovely, rapacious mouth from its gorging.
A head for bread, the barter system;
a whole life, halved. Extreme unction.

A body feels lighter that way. Delicate.
The guillotine, a simple palliative.
For even at the Queen's plainest–

a meadow garden with stream, ox-eyes,
cosmos, and butterflies–there was that
distasteful abundance of prettiness.

Monet's Egg Girl

I walk through the gardens,
knock on the back door.
Madame isn't ready
with the money, so I
follow her into the dining room.

———

She keeps her coins in a tin
like we do. I touch
a chair, the table. Once I saw
the moon, this color. I run
my hand over the cupboard, its
sunflower brightness. I could hide
one of the plates on the shelf
in my basket. For me. My heart
thumps, let me stay here.

———

The priest is right. There is an eternity.
A yellow that doesn't go gray.
But Madame Monet, pushing my
shoulders, says it's time for me to leave.

———

Be too eager, *le père* says, and you'll lose
the job you have now. *La mère* hoots.

———

In summer my face
is the color of a brown egg;
in winter, white.
I wear a dull gray dress with another
at home just like it for Sunday.

———

I ask *la mère* if I may have a yellow dress.
She looks at me as if I'm crazy.
Then, a pair of yellow stockings?
Pour la nouvelle année. Je t'en prie.
I've never pleaded with *la mère* before.

———

I dream yellow. Yolk yellow, without a raw
egg's stickiness. I dawdle at Monet's windows
as I pass by.

———

Chickens. Chickens.
I duck out of the hen house,
chicken shit on my shoes.
La mère plucks a feather from my hair.

———

Today Monsieur Monet says he admires
very much the colors in my banty red rooster's
feathers. And I, as bold as I'll ever be, I say
I adore his yellow dining room.
He doesn't understand. I mean,
Adore. He laughs. You have
good taste, he says, *ma chère* egg girl.

———

I put my hand to my chest.
My heart is beating hard.
And that is that. And that is that.
The sun in his room.

STALIN'S DAUGHTER
or: Who poisoned Stalin?

He orders by pointing–that man's sausage,
that woman's bread. I order the vegetable,
potatoes. "What's a matter," he says
across the table, "you on a diet?
Take my advice, eat. Fat on your bones
is healthy. You never know when
you'll need it." He rips his bread apart,
sops up the plate's grease, dabs fat
from his mustache, then eats
the sweet rag, chases it down
with a shot. He wipes his lips
with the back of his hand. His belch,
soft, like a cat's, jars only his shoulders.
"I don't care," he says, "what those bastard
doctors say. What do they know!"
I take a packet from my purse, God forgive me,
slide its little drawer open, offer him
what looks like a licorice. Smiling,
he presses the black spot to his tongue.

Three Faces

>from Katherine Turczan's Portraits from Ukraine

I see you, Jesus, in your sweet,
boy-mobster disguise, crowned by
the available fox-tail and canary grass wreath.

Nothing else, besides your bared,
bony chest, resurrected. The future,
in unenviable shoes, has come to kiss you.

What are you offering us now?
A gray angel to sit on our bed?
He's no comfort to the pregnant

young woman. His wings, stubs,
a lover fallen from heaven. A stud.
Soon with another mouth to feed.

This can be as frightening as the face
of your fifty-year-old bride, Jesus,
the folds in her un-kissed cheeks,

her black, clump-heeled shoes, smug
on the convent floor. Her curtains,
always white. Her lamp, filled with oil.

Not like Antonia, the black-market
butcher, whose hands are lard-white
from working in flesh and blood.

Akhmatova's Place

Ascending and descending,
a condition of survival,
out-bluffing doors
that open to another
closed door.

Walking, seeing
everything in a rush,
while seeing nothing.
Hearing the void.
Feeling it.

Not hopeful, not
hopeless. Haggard.
Grey as the Fontanka's waves.
Her thoughts kept
behind a forehead

in the city's pretty
heart, her
crushing home,
her eyes'
hooded domain.

Pictures From an Extinction: The Motherland

On the outskirts of Chernobyl,
the house of an old woman,
her father gave it to her
as his mother gave it to him,
the same wardrobe and same sofa,
the same embroidered cloth
—red and czarist—over the table;
in the middle, the same bowl,
veined gloom and hunger
in late afternoon.

*

Tree in the garden,
a hologram, a statue,
a white incineration.

*

A chain of people circle the tree.
They can't stop themselves from stripping
its harvest. A moth-and-spider-gauze
sticks to their fingers and lips.
They devour the apple flesh, spitting out
brown states of seeds.
The earth writhes.—How these people
hate their treasonous stomach,

its groaning, churring satisfaction
with juice and corrupt pulp,
as if they'd fed it something
they could live from.

*

It's the end of the world,
  half the people live
in Paradise. The other half,
  ash. It's the end
of a word, end of mercy.
  Zeus technology
pardons no human mistake.

Remember Jehovah the judge,
  Siamese twins?
On the one hand casting
  us out of Eden?
Even while his better half
  prepared a table for us
in the presence of our enemies?

      *

The leukemia ward in Kyiv,
a former palace, has these
wonderful European windows,
glass cupboard doors the nurse
unlatches and flings open.

Children, in rows
of white beds,
direct little wings
of fright in their eyes
toward the opened wall.

      *

Tree of life,
Menorah branches.
Apples and leaves,
Red and green threats.
In a white garden
The watchman's gone blind.

*

The old woman again,
reflected in her window,
a pose of eating;
supper, a collage on glass:
Scarfed head, the table's
midland, its cracked bowl,
the spoon in swollen hand—
whatever it yields,
steaming.

Mrs. Henike and Mr. Mendelssohn

"If you would, Mrs. Henike," Mr. Mendelssohn said
to me at 79 (formerly 103) Great Portland Street in London,
"please keep a cold pudding for me in my living room cupboard."
He liked my kidney pies, too.
"He would lift the crust," my Mr. Henike always said,
"and was tickled when the juice bubbled up!"

Did you know Mr. Mendelssohn kept two pianos in his rooms?
And a keyboard for his knees; in bed, he shut
his eyes to hear and played. Not a surprise, what
you'd expect of the great, the need to practice,
practice. For just look how a cook must work
to get things right. How many yolks separated,

how many cups of flour & treacle measured,
how many spins of the sifter and spoon before
she can get her kettle pudding great enough
to tickle a Mr. Mendelssohn. Genius, pure genius,
perhaps he said, I hope he said, opening the cupboard
at midnight, slipping his lonely spoon in. Unforgettable.

Dog Days in Court, 1780's, Berlin

—letters between Frederick the Great's sister Wilhelmina from her dog (Biche) to his dog (Folichon)

THEN, BERLIN

Though this letter be clearly written
in my mistress's hand, let it be known, I,

Biche, send you this history, Folichon,
recording the past, including our doghood

in Berlin, when we hid with them,
our masters, in the armoire and

your master Frederick comforted mine
under the odor of old robes—

*Don't worry, Mina, Father will die
some day, and then I'll be king.*

Your Frederick, nurturing two passions,
war and music. He disgusted his father

with his flute-playing. And my Mina
disgusted him with our presence.

As did the Queen. None of us knew
where in the palace Mother hid.

MY ARRIVAL IN BAYREUTH

In Bayreuth drunks threw up
civilly in corners, not on Mina's dinner

plates. They talked French, took tea
among the villa's tatters. Mina the bride

yearned for panes in windows, bed
hangings to keep out drafts, a table

and a chair. I, shivering, panted to see
your dear face again, and just once, not

a bone, but a bon bon to gnaw on.
Such a marriage, Mina's, bittersweet

as coffee and wild cherries.
How sweet to possess, Folichon!

Not that I'm a hedonist, but, oh!
for a hunk of braunschweiger from Berlin.

THE NEW MARGRAVINE'S REIGN

To celebrate the death of the old Margrave,
an era of frayed cuffs, Mina lit candles to him,

shocking her Protestant subjects
with extravagance, light and import,

evening salons, lively conversations
with Voltaire (who stepped on my toes).

While I sniffed the garden paths,
Mina fired her husband's mistress,

a Prussian, Miss von Marwitz–
never a tidbit from that hand!–

and curbed faux intellectuals
in her park's new Temple of Silence.

BETRAYAL

Yes, I know Mina allowed the editorial
backing your master's rival,

the Empress. Yes, I know
it was no tail-wagging time;

your Frederick circled his palace
raving, cursing the Empress,

a Catholic, an Austrian and worst,
a woman. The bloody, filthy rag,

printed in your duchy. How could you, Mina?
Father's laughing in his grave.

Mina and I shuddered over his letter.
A grotesquerie.

As in, *Father will die some day,*
and then I'll be king.

AFTERMATH, ENDURING LOVE

My dear, divine sister. Frederick's
reconciliation with Mina was ashen,

(foretold by us in letters). Dear Folichon,
berries redden here in Mina's gardens,

her carousel of light and sound is fading.
I forgive your master's teary rage,

gorging on Europe to fatten Prussia.
In this dozing Duchy of Bayreuth,

I accept your sweet paw in marriage
and vow my love till death. *Your, Biche.*

On Brothers: A Conversation Between Dorothy Wordsworth and Nannerl Mozart in the Afterlife

Mozart: It's an airy thing, gloating
over names Wolfgang
used to call me—Horseface,
My Liver, My Stomach, My Lungs.

Wordsworth: I was my brother's beloved.
He called me his Beloved.

Mozart: Names keep a place for us
on earth. In church books.

Wordsworth: He rested his head on my shoulder.

Mozart: Have you never traveled alone?

Wordsworth: Only in death.

Mozart: I play to my ghosts forever,
my martyrs to music, to Vienna,
to the carousel of events
on the Empress's calendar.

Wordsworth: William sang, "Oh, my dear, dear sister,
"with what transport shall I again meet you."
With the transport of Angel Wings, William!
On the transports of hope, I follow you.

Mozart: Wolfgang always said
the human voice is the greatest instrument.

Wordsworth: Newsprint? I stuffed it
in our window cracks.

Mozart: Mice. Mice pested Wolfgang in Vienna,
              in his apart-from-us.

Wordsworth: I slept with his children to be near William.
              I put down their upsets.

Mozart: I know the banishment of attics.
              The nicks on the walls. The markers.

Wordsworth: (leaning close) Do you hear your brother's voice?
              I hear mine in every line in my journal.

Mozart: I hear house as love.

Wordsworth.   Oh, my lines flew
              in rags and tatters,
              but on Sundays
              we fed on rapture,
              on Mondays, bliss.

Mozart: O Cara 'Armonia!

Wordsworth: It was given William to write the sacred.
              I was given ears, hands and eyes to copy

Mozart: to play!

Wordsworth: what he wrote.

Mozart: What he wrote.
              I do understand. We so anticipate

Wordsworth: his thoughts and moods

Mozart: we wind up quite unable

Wordsworth: to belong to ours. (laughing)
              I'm not thankless!

119

My two years at Grasmere with William
bloomed. My life's complete happiness.

Mozart: Sometimes music, too, can be a small box.

Music, I Must Have Music

(After "Kaffee, Kaffee muss ich haben")
for the daughters of J.S. Bach: Catharina Dorothea,
Elisabeth Juliana, Johanna Carolina, and Regina Susanna

Music, I must have music, you sang, stealing
to clavichords, the seven in the parlor,
seven, never enough, your seven brothers
were quite quick to lay their claim.

But where would Bach have put eleven
in his house? Its mornings cluttered,
competing with Zimmermann's,
a coffeehouse for music-loving amateurs.

Over the brook you stole singing, a flock
of larks, a clatter of cups, one quick jump
from Zimmermann's tables to his Klavier–
(Hey! Your father's calling.)–your romping

Musik, Musik, Musik muss ich haben,
splashing in it, music, I must have it,
laughing over it, I must.
      (Hey! Your chores
are calling!)
      Ah, there you go,

stealing away to the fountain, like any
homespun Leipzig girl in St. Thomas Square,
toting home the family's buckets of water.
Notes splattering under your quick steps.

Subjects (in four parts)

for Artemisia Gentileschi, 1593-1652

1.

As to the paintings, hers were a Baroque
kind of home therapy, vicariously
sizing up her rapist as if he were
a plucked chicken, wielding her
brush like a knife, rendering him
the enemy in the Biblical story,
"Judith Slaying Holofernes,"
dispatch the job, written all over
the subject's, Judith's, face, mirroring
the painter's. The virgin-white sheet,
speckled with blood. The rapist's fist
balled against the female breast,
ever so weakly, due to a deep slit
in his jugular. And yet, vengeance
can be delicate. Look how tenderly,
in the painter's *Jael and Sisera*, Jael
pounds a peg into her enemy's ear. Sleep.Tight.

2.

Maybe you call it lapis lazuli, maybe royal blue.
The fabric is rich as the first, unfolded evening
or premier gentian. Blue's throaty, trumpet voice.
Against a golden shift you have the stunning
first day and night in the firmament. You have
first cousin to the great. You have Judith,
in blue, her breasts slipping out of her bodice.

The heart beats wildly. Judith's maidservant
looks over her shoulder, fearing anyone
walking in on the act—catching the two women
carrying off Holofernes's head in a basket.

Such rustling satins, deep folds, dresses
as recitations of a story's favorite lines.
They do not want one single omission.

3.

A light meal with Giovanni Galileo and daughter.
Bread, cheese, olives on the table. The astronomer's
eyes, cloaked brilliance. He likes to hear the painter
talk about her work; he doesn't wish to see it.
She says she's sketching *Susanne & the Elders*,
but their heads are too cocked, they must seem
with her Susanne like the average authoritarian:
Two nondescript men from the same, small town,
their blood pounds harder, taking a virgin.
Tomorrow, before someone calls *Artemisia!*—before
the baby wakes, before a creditor hounds the door,
before her body demands she leave the easel,
she'll get them right. In mock practice, over her plate,
the painter's hand poses like an asp before the strike.

4.

Cara, the painter's self-portrait. She reassures
her skin she loves it still. Even after the rapist
has handled it, her body is the ever-present
model for a rounded arm, a shadowed eye,
which side of the face to reveal.

Her hand flies, at work even in sleep,
when she reaches for her man, his sex, she
weighs its bulge, measuring what might be
Holofernes's size. Would robes diminish it?
So the only blob one sees is his severed head?

Her stove, her oven, the strip between
her legs, she is the hottest woman in Florence.
No one dare touch her. Before she even

enters a room, she's already painting
her reaction according to who sits where.

The beauty of an inner room! Jupiter's
sperm sprays as stars through the portico's
windows. A golden storm. It catches
her breath. She paints Danaï,
the subject, catching the stars in her fist.

A Christmas Story...of a Sort

For behold, Erika's Christmas cactus blooms again,
long after her death and its journey to our house
from her apartment where the cactus flourished
in the room's desert air, the way some refugees
cross borders like years, arriving at a window
after a long, dark spell on a re-named street,

in denial of the room landed in, a firetrap
of cords, some snaking up a wall, some,
creeping along a baseboard; one, taped
to a table leg. On a hanger, a coquettish
white slip clung to the gray seersucker suit
found in the bundle from a rummage sale.

"I was frivolous once," Erika sighed as if
time were fragrant, or water, sipped from a china
cup in the German academy in St. Petersburg.
Oh, to stay in 1912. Decades before a stroke
did her in, before the world stood her up,
turned frivolous twit into *Putzfrau*, arched-nosed

bearer of an American rest home's shit pans.–
So who would have thought after a long,
silent exile, a flowering would return
to Erika's cactus with such éclat? Risen
on stems, dry as Jesse's root, belting out
protest at any absence of light in the world.

"Dear Little Sister"–Wil van Gogh

She is at home in a corner,
a witness to black roosters pecking
it out–Father and brother–flying
right at each other's eyes, a raw

defense. Why don't you leave,
Vincent? she whispers. Go.
Assimilate in the Bournasage
the browns in shadow and potato.

She, the nurse, paints in yellow
light awash in orange-blue.
It's in her blood, too, Vincent's
blue danger. She has that eye, too.

The patient she cares for is calling,
drowning the placid Dutch sky
and apple branch blossom in grey.
Sometimes she wishes she had no ears.

Wonder Woman at Seventy

for The Two Fat Ladies

No longer fitting into her hourglass costume–
valentine top and bottom–Wonder Woman
trades her bullet proof bracelets for a decent
lime squeezer and dons a smock in the kitchen.
Things don't die, only change.

Like "garlic and ginger, a lovely mixture"
improves a cut of meat. Ditto "beloved rosemary,"
tucked under a leg of lamb. The ending will be delicious.
All nettles extracted, all artichokes rubbed
with lemon so their tongues won't blacken.

Like God, Wonder Woman has very few vices:
The garlic, the rosemary, a tall glass of gin,
bacon, laid in union-jack strips over an otherwise
dry hen. Rule Britannia! Just pop into the oven.
The bird begins, throatily, to sing.

The Bird Men

    for Sterchens, Katherine Wright, Orv and Wilbur's sister

This thing of being bird-like, weighing
only fifty-two pounds: Their first glider
cost $15.00, a fortune spent on the uncertain.

This thing of dreaming like seabirds
on the wing, measuring wing spread,
multiplying it by six, both fore and aft

dimension, lateral surface not less,
not more than twenty. Small angles,
best for efficiency. This bird-like act,

henpecking every technique
for its truth, arched in a warp,
waiting for the right tap, the right twist—

what is crucial—equilibrium—preserved,
flying from gravity without gyring
into the galaxy of obscurity. This

bird-like flailing in high wind,
like a buzzard, slow and heavy,
a success that looks like failure.

               *

On the shifting sands of Kitty Hawk, on a finger
of sound built up between
the Atlantic and the mainland, on Kill Devil Hills,

in the undomesticated reserve

of Albamark, the wind
moved air and worry
like furniture around a room.

"Before you can fly, you must glide, Sterchens."

"Wilbur, Orv!
if you need to sew the wing, I'll show you how,
so you can sew it yourself."

Sky Is Great, the Sky Is Blue

2010

"... maybe, it would puzzle us
To find our way Home—" Emily Dickinson, #224

Along the Wall, Jakuba ul

I met the old woman who lives in Kazimierz
walking her small dog one evening.
She looked up long enough to throw me a glance.
How much you have, Foreigner, it said.
How is it you deserve two canes?
She wore a gray coat; the dog's was black.
The door they entered I'd call squalid,
the stairs they climbed looked to me like despair.

And yet the little dog's tail was wagging,
playing, as if a little higher, a little closer
to the sun, grey turned to silver, pallor
into rose, and the greatest happiness
that could befall them now
would be another centimeter of new snow.

Garden Scene

> *painting by Stanislav Zhukovski, 1873-1944;*
> *d. in Prushkov Concentration Camp near Warsaw*

The garden's divided in half by a picket fence.
On the closer side, a small table,
clothed and adorned by the useful
cup and tea pot, saucer, spoon,
painted in times when it was possible

to step into the house and find
a plate of bread to carry out.
To sit, to eat, to drink
under an awning of birch leaves,
near a flowerbed wash of swamp-red pinks.

Such a plain scene to fall in love with.
I want to gaze and gaze. A garden
in dreams from across a sea. It keeps
the heart beating in times of scarcity,
when a man became full merely by remembering.

Bells

Never whining after holing
themselves up in a tower for hours,

tolling
to the full
ends of their leashes,

not dwelling on their sounds'
sure demise.

Easily understandable.
Is as in 'just is.' So,

is.
Is as is.
Is.

Ringing,
clanging,

        over the park,
        across the gray, hobbled sky,

hoarse with amour,
trained to call,
Home. Home.

Tomatoes

Today I have eaten a perfect tomato.
A taste as singular as a voice, a full-
throated Russian soprano's, breathing
the end of summer and sunlight itself.
Nothing as social though as Mr. Neruda's ode.

Can I help it if I gorge on a second?
(In secret.) Or heighten, like a glutton,
the flavor of juicy pulp with salt?
Red, what I crave during winter, why
I dream of zinnias, their lack of discipline.

My Eden's apple, I eat you over the sink.
Childhood, granted a bit more sugar,
loneliness, plumped by sun and water.
Brilliant and common as the moon.
But much fleshier, much more human.

An Evening of Klezmer

for Tad; Kraków

Like a ghost town, the Jewish quarter,
where you can hear church bells ringing.
We didn't like being outside, alone.
We put our faces up to the paned
café windows and peered in.
Revelers sat around small tables,
walled in by drink and music.
A clarinetist played, moving
as if something long hidden
was being found. We wanted to step
inside where people were laughing
and clapping, but there was no room.
We hung around and waited,
watching for an opening,
but no one inside wanted to get out.

The Vistula

She is long and lazy. It's her toenails I see
flashing in the sun. A shiny paint job;
people love how she is old and young.

It's the same all over the world. An eye
falls on a spot along a curvy river and fifteen
thousand years later it's a city or town,

ruined several times over by war.
Once in a while not.
I saw a blue tent camping sleepily

on the Vistula's banks.
And Kraków's bridges
come from a hundred years ago.

Pattern

Alone at the window, its narrow glass doors open.
From a manor's grounds an old breeze spills in.
Lace curtains flow around the round table and lamp,
Maybe twenty, thirty, forty years old. I feel
Under the shade's fringed hem for the switch.
An amber stage appears on the table's cloth,
An audience of shadows, hints and intonations,
A vague sense of recollection, a touch of warmth,
A chance for anyone from the past to appear,
To walk into this dusk; alive, happy, talking.

On the Prairie:
Selections from

Love from the Yellowstone Trail, 2013

*Visibility Ten Miles: A Prairie
Memoir in Photography and Poetry,* 2015

The Sky Is Great, the Sky Is Blue, 2010

The Rhubarb King, 2015

"All of it happened slow …" Stanley Kunitz

First a River

1.

Glow of worn velvet. The West.
At twelve I wrote my name and age in its closet.
I knew its hills like friends,
how they change blue-yellow-green,
sentinels keeping time. I knew
dust in hair, shadows in a living room,
tragedies boxed and covered up, a warped
sense of possession. I knew how
in evening it cooled off–
some rest on the forehead,
some grace in quietness,
some darkness coming over its shoulder.
I've seen the river's plain table and its gifts
from the dead daughter, shells, birds,
the white tail that makes its way
through blonde grasses to drink at the shore.

2.

The mountains, too large to be called home.
You run from them for shelter in a town.
You dominate your life, your house, with kitsch.
As for the river, it's more modest,
it stays and it leaves.

Who can compare it to generations?
Made from a forked design–

the Madison, Jefferson, Gallatin–
its bed, brown as a trout or bullhead,
its water, green and blue. Jump two feet
and you've made it from bank to shore.

3.

Pebbles and dirt underfoot. Juniper
musk carried on a chill, May wind.
Here and there, coves along the river,
the charred remains of an evening fire.
Impossible not to want to light one,
if the creature you are is human,
if it's night, and there's driftwood
at hand, and you're with friends
or alone and you're listening
to the river, pocked with age, still
flowing indelibly by.

Fire and Water

This year the grass is so dry, a whisper
could set it off. Drought has descended

like summer snow, bleaching the grasslands
along the river, where, for a thousand seasons,

Mandans set the prairie on fire, loosed
the blistering monster to thunder over lives

of the slow-legged and gorge on grass.
Firefighters now, they rush in for a kill, aiming

for the carmine throat. They return home,
soot-faced, hands stuffed with money to burn.

*

We've penned her in, fattened her up, tamed her.
Named her 'reservoir.' All the cottonwoods

on her banks fall, choked with water.
Like corpses they topple, barkless, leafless,

covering themselves with the sadness
of water. Snakes, the harmless but ghastly

bull snakes, slither for cover. A ghost scene.
Scavengers drive out from town,

haul driftwood home, dowel it out
for trays, bowls, candle holders.

*

Citizens meet in the Wrangler, their arms folded
across their chests. They've been double-crossed

by the Corps of Engineers. The Brigadier General
has some explaining to do. They accuse him

of mismanaging the river, allowing in drought
too much water to leave her upper basin.

It flows downstream to fatten people's pockets
two states south. That isn't why farmers agreed

to give up the river for a lake.—It's come to this,
hot air and piss. No one goes home satisfied.

   *

She has a marina on the east, Jed's Landing.
Little cabins, cute cabins, you can rent.

Last year Lakotas bought the landing.
But what can they do now for a river's ghost?

Who would recognize her, slim and flowing,
her waves, oh,oh,oh,oh in places. She lies low,

looking at the sky, reflecting the blue
with deep bends. Never overflowing.

In the land's ravines, desire drums
for the wet fervor of the former lover.

   *

Thundercloud the rancher shows his neighbor
Joe Keller, a pyre where his Lakota mother

wizens under sun, the body in her slow return
to dust. Keller remembers "dust to dust"

from his own catechism, engrained
in a man with ten children. To him, we're all

Zachariah's shepherds on a thin shore, waving
our dried-up arms, railing at small currents

from large disappointments, excited and fearful
when fire ignites the basin of an ancient sea.

Love from the Yellowstone Trail

1.
The historical society meets for a picnic tonight,
6:00 to 8:00, Senior Citizens Center, in a walnut-paneled room
off Highway 12. When the conversation tires
of Barns Again! it drifts on to Lewis and Clark.
What was eaten on the long trek. Venison. Bear. Bear
is good if you know how to fix it. Otherwise, it's all fat.
And bison. Little-known to known facts get spit out
over bowls of spaghetti salad, baked beans and dark chips—
which could be something Lewis and Clark took along,
now couldn't it?—You take a bison, so much easier
to raise than cattle. And bison like to slide around
on an iced-over pond. No. Yes! What about buffalo fish?
Big-headed monsters, though they're not local.
Carp are. The woman who lived in New York City once,
whose Navaho earrings swing when she turns her head,
saw carp for sale out there. It's a delicacy out East.
She asked the vendor where it was from and he told her,
"From a place you've probably never been in, far away,
in South Dakota." Big laugh out of that
from the historical society in faraway South Dakota.

2.
Of everything Valerian Three Irons has said
under the Chautauqua tent, my sister found
his talk on Sacagawea's name most interesting.
(Though she nodded off on her folding chair,
and more than once watched the hills around us,
where wind runs in tall grass, sleek and invisible
as guilt up the spine.) Sacagawea, Shoshone
for "boat launcher"? Or Sacacawea–
the way the Hidatsas say it–"Bird woman"?

She was thinking about Mr. Tobin, she whispers,
his mnemonic device so powerful its spell rises
sixty years later on a clear August morning.
She raises her hand to recite it.
"S-a, c-a, g-a, we-a." My sister says it again
for its rosary of comfort. "Sacagawea."

3.
A train goes by, a long chain of wheat cars
and coal cars labeled Burlington Northern.
My sister and I stand in the gravel road
beside the tracks, counting and waving
as if we were girls again. She, old enough
to have watched Hunkpapa and Hidatsa
dance in full dress at the depot for tips.

And now Lakota have moved in next door to her,
in the rented house. A soap opera kind of life.
The young woman pitches his clothes—jeans
and cowboy shirts—into the driveway, the back-
door-bang **punc**-tu-**a**-ting each toss. Then he
catches her in an embrace, slowing down
the unconquerable with a kiss.

Old Glory Passes By

From a house on Standing Rock, lonely Highway 1806 South,
       the stars
and stripes flies straight over the rez, like the flag on the moon
       —Great Sioux Reservation created, 1868

and across the bridge, a regiment of West River ranchers on
       horseback
struts Old Glory down Main past crowds of folks who
       remove their hats
       —Custer violates 1868 Treaty in Black Hills, 1874

and clasp their hands over their hearts while white-ankled
       palominos,
chestnuts, black stallions clop by, tails swishing, flanks shuddering
       —Sioux must return to Reservation or be considered
       hostile, 1876

outpacing the floats, the rodeo princess candidates' and high
       school band's,
the class reunions' of '82 and '52, cluttered by brigades of
       small flags
       —Teton Sioux win Battle of Rosebud, 1876

ditto the law firm (Bettelspacher, Custer, Raabe & Red Hawk)
ignored by the young Lakota walking with his white girlfriend,
       —Lakota win Battle of Greasy Grass (Little Big Horn),
       1876

teens holding hands through a gauntlet of averted eyes and
the curb's dust devils, dervishes of butts and dust, grit
       —Native lands established as Indian Territory, 1882

that gets in your eyes, and the eyes of the Lakota kids
drumming for the 21st Century Community Learning Center
       —Native American religious practices forbidden, 1883

where Bullhead's office name plate reads Mr. Bullhead.
I like the horseman who's undone his braids, let his hair
      —Reservations reduced in size, 1889

bloom thick and black over his bare, ample shoulders.
No trace on him of Old Glory's colors. Look:
      —Ghost Dance Inaugurated on Pine Ridge, 1889

the Senate candidate's flaggy necktie and glory-gleam grin.
"No candy, no votes!" the voters half-joke, priming their kids
      —Massacre at Wounded Knee, 1890

to hustle candy from Mr. Thune and the '57 Buick convertible
hawking the August Lewis and Clark Festival. I squirm
      —Jim Thorpe (Wa-Tho-Huk) Olympic Champion, 1912

in the red-white-and blue matching socks and red USA T-shirt
my sister's bought for us to wear, Citizen Sister Twins.
      —Lakota warriors serve in WWI

Behind heartbreaker cheer leaders—ten whites, two Lakota
(a better ratio than in my day: 12 to null)—the Golden Oldies
      —American Indians become U. S. citizens, 1924

on the Care Center float, harmonizing to Johnnie Olson
on his synthesizer, get drowned out by the city's fire trucks,
      —Charles D. Curtis (part Kaw) elected Vice President, 1929

new and big-bucks yellow, a pair of wailing heroes
tossing sweaty kids more candy that rat-a-tat-tats
      —Lakota Code-Talkers serve under MacArthur, WWII

on the hot street like firecrackers under the Shriners'
swaggers, startling nobody when one falls off his go-cart.
      —Occupation of Wounded Knee, February-May 1973

The scat crew, all shit-eating grins, brings up the rear, shoveling piles of fresh horse apples perfuming lower Main. "That's it!"
 —Leonard Peltier convicted of murder, 1975

We fold our chairs and go on home in time for the family picnic, then sunset fireworks shooting over the Sitting Bull Stampede.
 —Year of reconciliation between American Indians and non-Indians, 1992

McIntosh, South Dakota

Outside the four-room house with porch and buckled walk,
a car pulls up on this Sunday noon, a Chevy, a '48 or '49.
The doors swing open; a man, woman and child in braids slide out.
The woman still young enough to have all her own teeth.
It's 1950 or '52, I'm guessing, for this isn't a photo, but memory,
not in sepia, but in gray. As for the jolly woman on the porch,

she's the man's aunt, beaming. His uncle, Fred, on the step,
operated a threshing rig with the man's father in the Antelope Valley,
before Fred became a heretic, got his worship day all screwed up,
turned Seventh Day Adventist, was banished from North Dakota
to Canada, Saskatchewan's wheat fields, then South Dakota's and now
his belly shows who sits in the living room waiting for dinner.

The aunt is wiping her hands on her starched and ironed apron.
The uncle extends his hand. Come in, come in, *Herein!*
The table is an offering, the bounty of reconciliation. First, steaming
soup, homemade noodles. Then mashed potatoes, beef, pickles,
garden lettuce drowned in cream, crust-cracking bread and *kuchen*,
heavy on whole cream, eggs and butter. Conflagrations of fragrance.

The onus is on the child at the table; of the five, sweating over
                their plates
of forgiveness, she will live longest. She's handicapped: she hasn't
the vaguest notion how anything is driven or made from scratch.
To her, things just are. She isn't even aware of her job, to hold
the memory as close as heaven, a history where they'll live forever,
warm and out-moded. A gray sort of comfort she'll find in the lost.

Two Voices from the Trail

1805

They don't see my lips moving when I answer their questions,
Charbonneau, Lewis and Clark. The answer's over and they haven't
caught it, the magpie, the voice of Three Sisters, the mother
ten thousand years old. Something marked but not bought,
spreading its velvet black tail with the convincing white streak.
A statement in shroud and revelation. Though they count my
hand when they vote in the encampment on the river, free-flowing,
narrow, swift in places. Lined by cottonwood groves. Water
for vast herds of game. Shelter for lodges with firewood at hand.
My son will become a Charbonneau with schooling. My daughter
stays at my side. At my dying when my sisters ask if they should call
my husband in, I'll shake my head. No. This last, quiet bed is mine.

2001

Under the thin blanket of the Milky Way and a starry
teapot, we pass the monument boosters built in the Twenties
to the only 'squaw worth living: She helped the white man.'
Does she sense us? On the road to Bullhead with our car full
of family, the way the present moves across the prairie. History
stirs in ravines. Darkness covers box houses, school,
the trading post. We arrive at the encampment on Rock Creek,
where "The mosquitoes have been put to bed," or so the KLND
announcer says. The powwow begins. No beatings tonight
in Bullhead. No one high on koolaid laced with hairspray.
More dancers than watchers. When we drive back home,
a moon-struck windsail surfs the waves of a once great river.

In Each Other's Hair

This took place long ago on a strip of lawn:
The seed blown in from who knows where,
for free. We needed rags (for curls)
so Ma ripped up a dish cloth, embroidered
muslin. My sister carried out the stool,
wooden, handmade for the kitchen. The dry,
summer, endless sky favored no one
below it though I was promised I'd be
beautiful. I brought my wet-haired self
and sat; behind me Ma unsnarled & wrapped
my hair for locks.—All was in the doing,
the going out beyond walls,
a caravan of three, bearing throne
and wrapping, comb and jar of summer
myrrh and hairpins. We set up camp
among lilacs, beside a bed of dusty mint.
Nothing of the afternoon was expected
to remain, not the tending nor the laughing,
nor the cups of love spent carelessly, as if it were
water and we lived in the shadows of a stream.

Lucifer at the Supper Table

"...from Morn to Noon he fell, from Noon to dewy Eve,
A Summer's day; and with the setting Sun Dropt
from the Zenith like a falling Star..." *Paradise Lost*

...and is sitting at my mother's table.
He has hung his hat on the corner of the door,
open to the breeze, *the breece*,
the porch door open to cool things down.

He eats like a German, mid-arms resting
on the table, spills nothing on his chin.
Should a pea roll from his plate, he bends
to pick it up, hemming himself into the tiny

kingdom he has landed in, our land
of stove, land of table, of big chair and radio,
four corners that can't accommodate
the spread of his wings; the dizzying

ivy wallpaper, fit only for a fly.
Our offerings, a platter of cold cuts.
He's handsome, my fallen father, looking
out of the photo as I am looking

in. We are as small as dolls,
the furniture has shrunk. His is the only
face that looks up from the table. His,
the only smile. It could be threatening. Or broken.

Notes from the Trail

1.

"9th of <u>October</u>, 1804
a windey rainey night, and cold,
So much So we Could not speek
with the Indians to day ..." (Captain William Clark)

    Clark's mechanics reminds me of my father's,
    whose journals I found, scrolled, eight
    in a tube, a record on butcher paper:

        "Oct. 1981 on the 9th
        after snowing 4 inchs
        a morning dove sang her song"

2.

"<u>February</u> 13th, 1805
I returned last Night from a hunting party
much fatigued, haveing walked 30 miles
on the ice and through Points of wood land
in which the Snow was nearly Knee Deep"   (Clark)

    Snow was always Knee Deep,
    swept into corners, until the first
    hint of good weather. Then came song:
    walking to the door, throwing it open.

        "Feb. 1984 20th

        I saw wild geese fly over the Oahe lake
        in a straight line and about close to a 1/4th of a mile long,
        they were headed north."

3.

"9th of March, 1805
a Cloudy Cold and windey morning wind from the North.
I walked up to See the Party that is makeing Perogues,
about 5 miles above this, the wind hard and Cold...
I wind to the upper mandan Village
& Smoked a pipe with the Chief and returned ..." (Clark)

    For whom does one take notes?
    If not for oneself, to prove to someone,
    you were here. This grafitti on paper
    turns to dust, too; possibly,
    your true dust in the universe.

"March, 1980 18th
we went to Kulm today and saw Ducks, medow larks, Crows,
Robins and a gopher ... north of Eureka we began seeing snow
and when we got to Kulm they had up to 4 feet of the white stuf
and melting, the town is quite flat and water allover ..."

4.

"9th of April, 1805
I saw a Musquetor to day   ..." (Clark)

    When a day turns aimless,
    as it can on the Plains' immensity,
    horizons incredibly distant,
    you can practice setting down
    your chair in the exact spot
    you picked it up from.

        "April, 1985 9th
        I did hear a medow lark
        across the railroad avenue."

5.

"20th of April, 1805
Saw several buffalow lodged in the drift wood
which had been drouned in the winter ..." (Clark)

> How comfortably death lodges in driftwood,
> a small version of the darkness we fear.
> The fall from the Garden. Providentially
> we land on our own two feet. Wide-eyed.

>> "April, 1985 4th
>> Ice on the Oahe ... is gone, saw a grackle
>> and short tail black bird on this day..."

6.

"19th of April, 1805
the wind so hard from the N.W. that we were fearfull
of ventering our Canoes in the river ... the Praries appear
to Green, the cotton trees bigin to leave,
Saw some plumb bushes in full bloom, ..." (Clark)

> That is the prairie, telling everything
> by its appearance, leaving nothing
> for the wind but to agree.

>> "April, 1986 7th
>> on this day i saw a gopher west of Hosmer,
>> this was not the striped kind also heard
>> a medow lark he sounded so good"

7.

"June 13th, 1805
My fare is really sumptuous this evening;

buffaloe's humps, tongues and marrowbones,
fine trout parched meal pepper and salt, and a good appetite;
the last is not considered the least of the luxuries."
(Meriwether Lewis)

> My father reminded us we ate like kings.
> Better. As for him, his mouth always
> wanted more, but his stomach said no.
> Many times, he disobeyed. It was his
> eyes that deceived him;
> ah, that bitch of a garden.

>> "June,1984 11th
>> Tomatos blooming"

8.

"July 16th, 1805
a fair morning after a verry cold night, heavy dew..."(Clark)

> You never know when summer will come,
> put its feet up on the table, stay awhile,
> long enough to know and love the place.

>> "July, 1985 5th
>> furnice came on this morning"

Variations on Water

It rains on paper and salvation when someone leaves
Bibles stacked on church sills and the window open.

The baptistery is our watery altar. Near the pulpit
Virginia Baum leads us on the organ over the waves.

Each voice, its own priest, each note rolling
from the River Jordan and spouting God's blessings.

The lights over the vanquished pews are crowns
illuminating the gospel from the Sea of Galilee.

On the upper floor, in sleepy classrooms,
stories run like rivers through Jerusalem's alleys.

Jesus, the sweet drop of water in the desert.
Jesus, the living water from the Nazarene's well.

We are rowing in our little, pie-in-the-sky church
off the Yellowstone Trail bordering North Main.

We are rowing, but it gets harder; nowadays
the second floor is boarded off with sheet rock.

A wall to save on fuel. A door in case of emergency.
The preacher's day job is teaching high school.

We are rowing past last Sunday's catastrophe,
the collection's drought, eight dollars and a quarter.

When the Communion tray comes clinking down the pew,
we lift a thimble glass of grape juice and drink in remembrance.

Milton on the Plains: the Coal Furnace

> "A Dungeon horrible, on all sides round
> As one great Furnance flam'd, yet from those flames
> No light, but rather darkness visible
> Serv'd only to discover sights of woe ..." *Paradise Lost*

Like Milton's ours burned with unholy light.
My parents fed it in our basement's dusk,
two shadows banking darkness. Mom in gloves
and housedress, would heft a shovelful of lignite
to horrid lips and shove it in. Then clang!
The iron firing door slammed shut. Upstairs,
we walked the floorboards hearing smoldering coals;
trip on a floor vent, the fall burned like hell.
Imagination's fuel. A dose of Poe
ignites the tale: a heart that's ripped in two,
a night of drunken fury, a man who feeds
his wife to flames, limb by bloodied limb.
And who would stop her husband's deeds of woe?
His children? Hell's walls hold in the screams.
No one will search its ashy pit for bones.
The devil's throbbing anthem rings, Forever
Together.
       I prayed for a deliverer,
someone to tame the furnace, seal it up.
Hammer racket would convert it
to lighter gas or oil, a furnace fed
by tubes no man could shove a body through.

Another Love Letter

Irene Hartland, Dad. You could have had her by the looks of this photo.
Nice legs. Her silk stockings glare in the sun.
She's interested—standing beside you, curving in. The other girl
(my mother) on the left is too nice. Forget her. Irene is the one.
She likes your tender bulk in that winter coat with its fur epaulets.
She likes the sweater you wear underneath, and the way the collar
stands up like a prince's ruff around the back of your neck.
Consider her name, Dad. "Hard land." You'll be reasonably happy.
She's a German Russian, too, she understands how to handle
men like you.

No, not Irene? How about "Maggie?" Or Miss Fay? Or Miss Moon?
Tête a tête in the photo, your arm around her, you're bending down,
your six feet toward her, a wicked, sexy grin on your clean-shaven face.
Dad, stop right there. I'll go back to the universe and wait another round.
I herewith consign my sisters to the same, we slide gladly out of the picture.
For you. For Vila Netz. Or the Billigmeier girl. Either of the Miller sisters.
They all have a crush on you, your sunglasses, round as quarters.
Remove us, your daughters, and you're a frat boy, a movie star,
advertiser, salesman, efficiency expert from 160 acres in North Dakota.

Look at you now!
You who would not listen. You are a big,
lumpy walrus, old, wearing a cap labeled Sitting Bull Stampede.
Smiling because you've found three women who can live with you
underwater for an hour at a time. Your arms slide easily around us,
your daughters, your girls. Where you've taped this photo
into the album, I find two of your gray hairs. Two from the grave?
I almost pull them out, and then realizing it's too late,
I let you be.

Note: Germans who emigrated first to the Volga or Ukraine, 18th century
on, and then emigrated to the U.S. are often called Germans from Russia to
distinguish them from the Germans who emigrated to the U.S. directly from
Germany. They are not Russian nor Ukrainian.

Now It's Late

afternoon, rain runs down the folds in the plastic awning
over the front step. Conversation's left for its holy house,
quietly closed the door, following a path love made long ago.
Or was it duty? House clocks tick, the cuckoo, a beat ahead
of the grandfather. Four ticks to each ha-rumpf.
May air dozes in the living room after dinner
with a man and woman, fallen asleep sitting up.
The man's hands lie open on his leg and armrest,
great, wide paws, felled by sleep.
He nods defenseless, his head, a pompadour under snow.
The woman sits in her green-padded rocker,
her head slumped on her chest, gasping, now and then,
as though someone's just stuck her with a pin.
She almost leaves sleep but drifts back down again
to rest in the parlor of the sleeping kingdom.
Angers lie about, old smoke still adrift over the carpet.
Blame has curled up, its head on the sofa's pillow, its face
young again in sleep. Where's the prince who must come
to kiss old lips? Maybe he's fallen short of reaching the door.
He and his horse, under the spell; the house, unwakeable?

Fruit Closet

Is it right to spend time dwelling on an old fruit closet and
    its door handle?
(A homemade cross-bar holding two doors from flapping
    open, swinging out.)
Is it wise? To want to remember, keeping it just as it was, like
    something rich,
but, really, an awkward armoire, painted 1920 movie star
    green, thin-walled,
made by a father, its shelves two and one-half feet deep, a
    sturdy box,
set off the earth floor on wooden blocks. By summer's end,
the storehold of gleaming jars, specimens
under glass, skinned pears, peaches, crabapples,
sweetened for the winter table.
"Take home more," my father moans after my mother's death.
"I can never eat all of it up."
Apples, chokecherries, tomatoes, rhubarb, plums, cherries,
    jams, jellies,
spiked by the inevitable, bad jar that popped in the back.
    Spewed its fumes.
(She could have put her foot down and said, "No more."
She could have turned from the sink when he towered in
to the kitchen with his bulging handfuls of tomatoes,
    beginning the canning season.
"Why continue this?" she could have said.
"We will never eat this down. The past is already too full.")
Canning is a historical act, once common and cyclical,
performed by my mother's hands,
which neither death nor new ways changed;
they were the only part of her that looked real before the lid
    was closed.

In Ascent

My name is bird.
Here is my creed:
to fly, to glide, to hover,
to dip and wheel, to soar.
I change in light,
my color born of snow.
I move by light.
The evening stills me.
Here is my comfort:
my strength, my weakness,
my cry, my song.
I can't tell where
it begins or ends–
in the rabbit's gut,
in a cloud's moods,
in my wings at night.
I ascend and descend.
I light. I live.

How Do We Live in Winter Without Zinnias?

Winter's flowerless unless you count ice
crystals, more spoor than seed;
they do not perpetuate themselves.
Flower isn't as perfect a word as summer.
A summer, not as perfect as a zinnia.

Monday, from the elevator, I saw a woman

hunched over in her wheelchair, fallen asleep.
No. I'll think of the summer pot of flowers
awake on my table: zinnias, asters, gladiola,
straw and strawberry flowers, daisies
(white and lavender), and one rose dahlia.

Mr. Schmier's Wife

Champion of high-rising potato bread.
Her bosom, big as baskets under her apron.

She kept her parlor cool and neat.
At her fingertips, *National Geographics*

offered a variety of continents
and women, some with proud,

plate lips, some with long,
vase-like necks, some with breasts,

mahogany cups, perfectly tipped.
But what Mr. Schmier's wife

liked best was the little stoves
those women baked round breads in.

Wax Cylinder Recordings from a Small Town (7 parts)

1. A Shirt to Wear

She rode into town, ignoring the warnings. Streets, blocked,
traffic, uncertain. Ice on the Missouri, thinning.

She had my sister down under her apron. She didn't know,
not at all, the Deloria Sisters from across the river,

the reservation where they buried Sacajawea,
hunting grounds for Episcopalians. Ella Deloria

wrote a history of the Sun Dance; her sister
Susan preserved a Ghost Dance shirt, made holy

by the massacre at Wounded Knee. It was old
muslin, frailer than tea towel, the designs, worn

as a voice on a wax cylinder recording,
magic coming over waves of misfortune.

She didn't know this down in the basement,
sorting piles of whites and coloreds to wash.

Chipping away at a cake of lye, she couldn't detect
art work in work shirts, stiff with unblessed sweat.

2. Did You Hear That?

The ultimate, airy banister for small things–
a canister zipping down a pneumatic tube

from the mezzanine–wheee!–to main floor
in J.C. Penney's, carrying change to a clerk,

who never noticed her own hands, precise,
ringing up a sale, say, of a prom dress. She

withheld her opinion on how much you spent.
Started working at Penney's in the Twenties,

had to; still on her feet in the Fifties,
Sixties, Seventies. About her, the darkly sweet

fragrance of the weary. A company woman.
She covered her mouth when she coughed,

lower case coughs,
small as the *c* in scraping by.

3. Response to "Letters to the Editor", Found Poem

"What difference does it make
if we/ *Tribune* misspelled Sakajawea ...

we shall now call her Bird Woman...
she may also be called Mrs. Charbonneau

with a considerable degree
of propriety ... this means less

wear and tear on our spelling,
enunciation and pronunciation

apparatus, as well as upon the delicate
mechanism of our linotype

machine and the nervous system
of its patient, long-suffering operator."

4. The Sixth District Women's Convention

She thumbed her nose at the ladies
from her washer in the basement.

She was as pretty, and surely as quick
as an Honorable Mention, and at times,

as desperate as the ladies for something
other than dust, but she'd married

a peasant. Handsome, but sorry, wrong
class.—As if she were interested

in lawyered, doctored, business-manned
wives. As if she wanted to join their clubs,

the Cultus, the L'Eclatant Douzaine,
chicken-saladed, pink-tableclothed

gatherings. As if she wanted to listen
to Mrs. Cott's "My Trip to Rothenburg,"

or hear some heavy-chested canary
warble Wagner. His *Dämmerung*.

5. Drive

The new woman drove, unlike my mother.
A free woman like Maude Caldwell, owner

of one of the town's first five automobiles;
free to keep her first name after "Mrs.," have accidents,

leave town, spend the winters in Minneapolis.
Maude did perms. If the client's husband

was short of cash, he could work off the cost
in or outside the shop, a place

so small when Maude did Mrs. Batteen's
river of hair, she had to keep swaying

back, back into a closet to comb
to the end, the soft, brown waves.

Handsome, willowy Mrs. Batteen,
mistress to the richest man in Walworth County.

Her hair, heavy in Maude's hands, almost as heavy
as her lover's name engraved on the public

library's lintel. Never short of cash,
that one, Maude'd say, as she drove by.

6. I Get Her Name into Print

Ella Grace Clara,
speak from the cellar,
what is your counsel for me?

—*Be happy.*

7. Other Women

Other women worked in a cabin in the willows
along the river, their nipples, targets,

little bombshells for drunken johns
with pistols. Mae West lookalikes,

coming in sweet, Five-and-Dime perfume.
Their scarlet lipstick planted untidy O's

on married men's collars. (One stain
led to another to be washed in the cellar

with work shirts, slow to take offense.)
After the town routed out the West End,

whores scattered like cats down alleys,
so mangy they became police notes

in the Tribune, under the rung where names,
approved by the County for relief,

clustered in chilblained lists. I could go on,
but you see. The past falls, like a descant

from Eden. Voices get lost. Mrs. Bachelor,
our kitty-corner neighbor, whose kitchen

shone cloud-white, told my mother, "Ella,
heaven and hell are right here on earth."

View from Porch

Last week a storm took down an apple tree,
its shade over the porch
from the western sun,
and its bonus, apples.
It left behind space to see
to the very end of the yard.

There, clearly, The Little House sits.
An innocent face of corner windows,
side door, bordered by lilies and mint.
My sister's first house when she married.
Now it's summer kitchen and storage.
It could be more but isn't.

She's clearing it out slowly, an act,
I think, of unnecessary hastening,
to spare her daughter the final cleaning.
Masses of hollyhocks, brown-eyed Susans,
moss roses and petunias volunteer
to brighten the unused, gravel driveway.

The sweetest of morning breezes
blows through the porch screens.
We eat a light breakfast, like ladies,
at a table painted cheery yellow.
The wind chime shivers. "It feels
like fall," my sister breathes.

We sweep away the lengthening
shadows, their wintry signs,
into one of mind's back corners,
preferring to stay in morning,
its own screened walls calling,
"Come in and abide all summer."

Burning

"...I don't want to be burned." Louise Glück, "Averno"

Ah, but I want to burn, the way the field, the strong field,

the known field is burned in fall and spring in anticipation,

oh, much quicker than the slow clearing of flesh from bone.

Burned, loose from its scaffolding, flesh is a change into light,

into motes, scattering, over field, dust, catching in air, once

every winter I see this play as snow descends on a field

and its field tree, *gloriosa et immaculata*, and the joy

watching that change. I stand in the field by myself. At home.

You had children, I had none, I have no one to show the field,

or tell I'm sorry, or call and ask if they are lonely,

I have something to give to nothing; call me a show-off, call me

willing to cut off my nose ... when it comes, I'm ready to burn,

free of all boxing or packaging, it won't last long, that heat, that

singeing intensity on the flesh and then, the vibrant exit into wind.

The Beekeepers (5 parts)

pen and ink drawing by Pieter Bruegel the Elder, 1560's

1.
Such beings! Hooded. In place of a face a basket
mask, a snoutless countenance, flat as an idiot's,
round protection woven from the medieval mind.
No iron visor necessary, no bee can penetrate
that hemp surface. But how can the keepers
breathe behind it? How can they see?
                                                It's sure
they've walked the path so often between meadow
and hillock, they can do it in their sleep, ditto tying,
sightless, their sock-like shoes and habit-robe,
a cross between a monk's (with slit in side) and stalking
ghost's. En route, they step around the magnificent
skunk cabbage Bruegel's drawn. The bees may be
the dashes swarming into millions of June leaves.

2.
Their voices, muzzled. Their thoughts
reduced to mime and habitual movement.
Their heads buzz from the breakfast beer,
or the beer drunk last night to cool off
before they crawled, sweaty-haired and
sweaty-faced into bed, like bees crawling
into their hives, vincible, striking by instinct.

3.
What I'd thought was skunk cabbage is mandrake.
Mayapples is another name, a prettier reminder
of the scene from Eden. Beekeepers descend
from that nameless cousin who didn't eat of the apple.
God kept her in another part of the Garden.
She never questioned a bee's will.
Nor doubted a sting could hurt or kill.

4.
A bit like robbery or rape, the beekeepers' work,
and a bit like dance, slow, so as not to stir the bees.
The hive's the body their arms encircle,
a cone shape, squirming inside like a pig.
To take the honey, they plant both feet firmly,
tuck the buzzing cone between the legs, and
with claw-like fingers—or are they more like roots—
pry open the lid. There's little chance of feeling
stings through their enormous, padded shoulders.
Afterward, the hive's left lurched in the grass.

5.
Like love. On the losing side you take on hemp's armor.
You must agree losing something sweet could wreck
a face and turn it into unreadable flatness.
                                                        The world,
too, turns flat. Somewhere, even now, in a field,
a couple with one body jerks and moans,
as indivisible as honey from a comb.

6.
Then one stands up and one becomes two. And one
by one the two walk in opposite directions
home. One might say change is good; one, that
it's lonely. For bees and keepers, parting,
or its effort, is sticky, hard to do without
protection. Do you hide from the face you sting?
Or, stung, wear a basket? But how to breathe
through that tight cover? How to love what you see?

WOUNDED KNEE

What the eye holds, the heart holds, the ear holds.
Fourteen miles west of Philips, South Dakota,
on Interstate 90, I'm listening to W.A. Mozart,
a piece written in Salzburg, the Badland's baroque
coming up fast, *mako sica*'s pink architecture,
wind bridges and spires. Static making the music
ever more alien. I'm passing a herd of black angus,
Z Ranch Z's burned into hide. Whoever's
smelled a branding has an inkling of the air
near Auschwitz and Dachau, in Murnau
when the wind blew west. Burned flesh.
Singed hair. Such grief. Mozart would never.
His own set of inherited prejudices would be
ripped to the core: How could honest Germans?
Here the sky is so open it hides the stench of old massacres.

Haying

for Drew and Britt

Summer's ebbing. Grasses wallow around the field tree
where the tractor's discs can't reach, where shade

thins and folds. Under the sun, the necessity
of a water bottle. Or at the century's turn, a jug, a brown

ceramic jug from Ukraine, seen in Soviet Realist paintings:
laughing farm hands on a mid-morning break: bread, radish,

and water, water the unmarried sister lugs out to the field,
its chaff and heat. The sun, at a zenith in a painter's blue sky.

This business is for horses, this discing, cutting, baling.
The field's and the tractor's revolution make good money

some years. Blunt and brusque, the tractor's blade
uncovers a world of slithering snakes, pheasant chicks,

red fox, and the grasses' nomadic fragrances. It leaves
wakes of mown hay. Bales float to the horizon.

On the shore, the different world of house.
The tractor's the only ship on the Ocean with a Tree.

The Accent on Flat

Flat, the land is flat.
Like our accent—our r's

growl as they circle their
nests in the uvular cave.

Our eyeballs flatten, staring
at this sheet of land. Even

the voice, exalted in the vault
above the tongue, in

imitation of heaven, even
the voice goes flat.

And I think of certain women
as worn-down mountains,

women who set their
hearts down to sing.

Lilacs

A bouquet of lilacs, big as a bush,
lush, rich, a translation from Tristan
and Isolde's purple song of tumescence.
In my room, present as inheritance,
a fragrance in remembrance of flesh.
Only the sidewalks' neighborliness
restrains the lilacs' opulence, their
relentless busty business, the noise
they make in the street, their genius
favored by gods of scent and color.
Even in an old bush brittleness breaks out
of its gooseneck pattern to become a stroke
we love to feel on our lips and neck and thighs.

New Water

for Archie and Sharon

All those years—almost a hundred—
the farm had hard water.
Hard orange. Buckets lined in orange.
Sink and tub and toilet, too,
once they got running water.
And now, in less than a lifetime,
just by changing the well's location,
in the same yard, mind you,
the water's soft, clear, delicious to drink.
All those years to shake your head over.
Look how sweet life has become;
you can see it in the couple who live here,
their calmness as they sit at their table,
the beauty as they offer you new water to drink.

Zippers

I had a seamstress friend who spent two years in Hamburg
doing buttonholes. Once the buttonhole was conquered,
—my kingdom for a buttonhole—she moved on to design,
looking down her nose at zippers, their tiny levers
and steel tracks. Such is the demand of art: an arachnid
stitch, leaving a silken trace across cloth.

You need a northwest wind to test buttons vs. zippers,
the Palisades' breezes won't do, a bigger blast is called for,
a wind in which your appearance means nothing. Let two
men stand on a butte near the Missouri. Whose coat keeps warm
as a rabbit in its burrow under snow? Whose lets in a chill,
eventually splits, frigidly revealing the solitary chest alone?

Everything

At the corner of Cain's and Molstad's,
I turn west toward the river, following the tracks

to the viaduct, where the smell of creosote
seeps from the pillars and dirt bolstering it.

I skip from railroad tie to tie, my legs, surly.
I imagine a diesel coming, the pounding rails;

me, the coin, squashed flat. In the whistle's
blast, my mother's *Stay away from the tracks!*

I take the rest of my life left and leap
backwards, off the rails; now they lie

shimmering in summer heat and silence.
Grasshoppers fly at my jeans, snapping, loud

enough to be a good scare. But they are not
rattlers. I wade through weeds and blown paper

to a dirt road, a valley of ruts and grooves,
to Schlecht's, a house with encampment,

ramshackle as a stable with wing-additions.
A scrub tub squats on the open stoop.

And there stands Mrs. Schlecht, shaped like the rain
barrel, her face white with heat, her hair limp.

In her kitchen I drink syrup from canned pineapple,
then head back home, having tasted the world.

The Widow's House

2015

" … *caves offered no thrill for him. Much warmer, making his way through the darkness inside me.*"

Soon You're Free

a. At the Mandarin Restaurant: Take Out

This one has altars to threshold gods,
red, proscenium stages on inch-high platforms,
the smell of mint and basil above the dreck
customers drag in on their shoes.
One woman offers salad to her mate. Her rose
lips open as he takes a bite. Please,
Anonymous God of Coincidence and Goodness,
protect them from the days to come
when an old woman batters down
their door and insists she take over the house.

b. Chinese Take-Out for the Man Who's Had No Appetite for Weeks

He will eat at the table. He insists, he will
get out of bed and eat at our table. Heartily.
What a pun, made by a man with a bad ticker.
And he reminds me he wants hearty sandwiches
served at his funeral. Turkey, ham. Wheat buns.
Not a tray of almonds and cookies. Hearty!

c. From the Little White Boxes with Wire Handles

which include four packets of soy sauce,
brown as hemorrhage on his bathroom wall.
He reaches for a packet, and, as in a dream
he told me about, where he reaches out to me
and calls my name, and I do not answer,
sauce splatters all over his fingers.
"I didn't squeeze it!" he protests. I jump up
for wet toweling; we go on eating
in the style of last meals, when old
combatants make peace over dirty plates.

d. Fortune Cookies

He likes them. So do I.
He eats his with the rice and sauce.
He eats mine, too. Bites down.
Crunch.
Hey, that's mine, I say.
He stops munching.
Oh, go ahead and eat it, I say, but read me my fortune.
Long monologue, mine, as he unfolds the little scroll,
how they're not fortunes, but maxims, kitschy philosophy
with winning
lottery numbers. Not what I want to hear.
His hands are slow.
"Soon you're free," he finally reads, and goes on eating.
Really? Does it really say that?
He nods. He hands it over, across the table,
my slip of fortune, soon-you're-free, spelled as
Sympathy.

At His Bedside

I, the wife, inefficient nurse, former lover, express
          service toting parcels between
          home and hospice, praying
          to his mother, You, you had
your delight, now it's time to take him back.

He, the body in bed, ravaged, grotesquely swollen, each
          member imitating his enlarged
          heart: his scrotum, a pink
          pumpkin, his legs, purple
stumps, his feet, his poor, lovely feet, blocks. Now

I bend down to him, head to head, my cheek
          against his, clean, still sweet-
          male smelling, all the dregs
          of marriage drained away, only
after-ardor remains. And then the interloper

arrives, the third party he doesn't fear, the lure that
          sets his face alight, his
          breath like a boy's, running
          in gasps, as if he can barely
believe the beauty of the girl knocking at his door.

Talk

To say something and have someone
near enough to hear, even comment,

something small, like, "It's windy out"
when closing the bedroom blinds for the night–

what was once so possible, common,
redundant, seems to be now some

passionate miracle. Tomorrow,
the woman standing outside the church

told me, tomorrow is Divine Mercy,
tomorrow doors will be unlocked.

Tastes (in eight parts)

And if the bread wanted to be
a house—some loaves do

bear a resemblance—
how could you dissuade bread

that its lightness equals
a window light's welcome?

A crowd's already gathering
in the street; a house of bread,

confusing. Look what happened
when a woman built hers

of butter and sugar. The crumbs
of lives left over!—And all

for a wish of the impossibly
vexatious full moment:

making of stone, a leaven,
making a house rise on a corner.

∂

It was part of being noon
on earth, his hunger,

which, after minutes,
could feel immediate

summer and within
hours, return to winter,

barren, flayed thin,
impatient at the table,

a time-swept moor
of days, of months

when I didn't love him,
didn't always want

him. I haven't
mentioned that

he liked, at the sink,
to kiss my hair.

∂

In the cemetery, the dead
have such a slow way

to spring a surprise.
Ever since the snow

eased, I'd futzed about
their graves—set and clear,

set and clear.
In October, I visit,

and three lush graves
greet me as if I'd walked

in on their party, the father
speaking Polish; the mother

German; the son,
the middle man between.

I'm the lone guest
at their table, the silent one.

∂

In a restaurant with many windows,
the angel of the envious

flutters above two lovebirds.
Look away, look away, she whispers

to the woman sitting solo at a table.
Lift your eyes, she says,

to a nice glass of afternoon.
Drink to bristling motel managers

and their *Quiet down in there*-s
and to your devious assurances

to turn down the TV
which wasn't on.

Drink to your lover, sweetly
indignant at paper-thin walls.

We're such old fools,
the angel quivers.

∂

Sometimes end-stops take a long leave of absence
before they grace the right side of the white page,

the heart pumping door slams.
Halts. Marks. Dots.

Dot. Not period. A short
story contains twenty? fifty?

periods. Plus the I period.
The He period. The She period,

when more than once ... oh, he
was freshly showered and interested ...

cheeks shaved, shining ...
hair still wet but combed ...

dot, dot, dot,
his clean white T-shirt off,

tap, tap, tap ... the entire
violin section tucked in their chins.

∂

The taste for sweet, for salt,
for love lies in the buds

of a slick organ. Being
mammal, a licker

and a sucker with a bent
for confection, I

prefer frosting, cream,
the oil on his skin,

a remembered presence
my tongue so

admired
on its small

maneuvers over
the close,

the desirable,
I could go on.

∂

Alone, that word
and its gang,

forlorn, wan.
They're all a ruse,

a curse,
a boomerang.

It can be said
passion is unhealthy.

Turn the page,
the orchard's ripened.

Turn the page,
the cat's circled thrice.

Turn the page and
you see autumn

in water, the wind
solo and always solo.

∂

On the street of the sea
of God's miracle, everything

happens in squares and doorways.
Especially in evenings and late afternoons.

Kept, kept, what a beautiful word,
as in *they belong, they have a home.*

His isn't a great song in the lane, the workman's,
just as his isn't a great love, but listen to him sing.

In our separateness, my love once said,
we found our togetherness.

!Hola, Hola! is a greeting made
by blowing a kiss over vowels

and walking on, a direction
leading out of the old. At # 56

a woman unlocks the door
with the blue key and walks in.

A Widow's Tale, As Ancient As Can Be

On his wedding day he'd asked himself what
was he doing. But he drove on to the church.
A mistake, he said later. But who can trust
what a frustrated man in a pique says?

Besides, aren't lies part of a happy occasion?
If everything about love is a lie, does it matter?
Aren't the contents interesting? Love becomes
a repository for the Alone One later to open.

The light fell so wonderfully shadowy over
the table set by the lake. As the afternoon
wore on, the couple were coaxed to eat their cake.
June was in its quiet mode, young and confident.

As was the pastor, calling out the bride's new name.
She looked to her mother-in-law to reply.
Everyone laughed then, including the bride,
catching herself as wife, a curious pang in her chest.

Elegy in a Single Bed

And I remember your shoulders,
their strength then and their curves,
your torso, its tautness,
its funky sweat during love,
your bare buttocks, hard,
and the back of your thighs,
I remember your chest
and abdomen, and the points
underneath I remember
with pleasure your weight
against me, with my eyes
closed I remember and all
the feelings and pressure
I've recorded, embedded
in the skin of my fingers.
Was I bamboozled?
Isn't love everything?

The Bottom Rung on the Social Ladder (Well, Just above Bingo): Watching Love Movies on a Friday Night, Alone

It's 1937. Young Cary Grant and Irene Dunn
are luckily happily married in *The Awful Truth*
until they split. What caused it isn't important
here. Just know that before the divorce, they have
everything. Love, money, sex, terrific apartment,
maids, a non-interfering, sophisticated aunt,
an ultra-smart dog (Mr. Smith), liked even by dog haters.
Who in a depression wouldn't want to be them?
Then the searing separation. It's hilarious—
Cary's missteps, Irene's mishaps, I nearly split my
gut pretending you're in your place on the couch,
and it's our Friday night date. You're looking at me
to see if I'm laughing as hard as you, and I'm looking
at you to see if you like this because I like it so much.
But I'm crying because it isn't funny that I have to pretend,
and I'm aching for Cary and Irene to get together
again, when finally, at the eleventh hour,
wily Irene plays her last card so to speak,
landing them in a mountain cabin. Well, they go to bed,
separate bedrooms, but neither can sleep and I
couldn't either in a similar situation, my juices
would be running, my tongue twisted like a
pretzel over whether I should call him in. (Yes.)
Meanwhile, the shutters are banging in a storm,
a door's creaking, the camera pans a black cat,
a cuckoo clock, all irrelevant, all red herrings
to keep Cary from jumping into Irene's bed
(though what keeps them apart gets them together:
nice paradox and use of device and object,
but who cares about the literary bullshit), I want him
sliding into her, finding her wet and marvelous,

and I want them to feel each other in a way only
sex can make you feel after a long absence.
And I know, I hope, they do, it, though anyone
watching isn't exactly sure because the camera's
eye swings back to that cuckoo clock, a mock
German weather house where a man in Lederhosen
and a woman in a Dirndl go in together on the hour,
which is a nice way to say the f-word.
Thank you, Special Effects. If you were here,
you'd be cheering, "Kiss her, kiss her," and I'd
pretend it wasn't because Irene is so gorgeous,
but because you love me. And we'd know
the ending was going to be happy, if postponed.
And I'd know what was so awful in a split was awful
if, come morning, they could never kiss alive again.

Purgatory

is love and sensing the departed is present
somewhere between being able to be
reached or not. Neither alive nor dead.
It is searching hopefully for him,
in the pew he used to choose, mid-way
between altar and exit. It is listening
on All Souls' Day to Mozart's Requiem
while writing the deceased's name
on one of the small, pink envelopes provided
and sent up to the priest who'll pass his hands
over the basket making magic, making all
who are away know the living still pay them
attention and oh and oh and oh and oh. *Voca me!*
It is leaving, walking down the mountainous
terrace of concrete steps and turning back to
look at the church on a mild November evening.
It is knowing the other, the Away One, was
there, unseen, and, as ever, waiting. It is pretending.

Goodnight

for Tad

If you can see me now, you'll notice I've barricaded myself
behind a stack of books on the footstool. Magazines on my right,
newspaper on the left. When I finish reading, it'll be time for bed.

The month, half gone; the moon outside the couch window,
full and glorious. You're still getting phone calls; just now,
a young woman. She's politely sorry when I tell her you are dead.

Having worked phone banks, I know she's checking a box
labeled D for deceased. You'll not be called by her again.
I'm glad the moon is out. I hope you can see it.

It's getting dark early now, and colder. Settling in,
sliding forward. A peasant. Her scruffy cart.
Tomorrow I give your winter coat and hats away.

On Green

> Green, how I want you green.
> "Verde, te que quiero verde." Lorca

And I walked into the garden, the
underfoot rough with stubble weeds
and dirt. Under the pepper tree I walked,
under its silky negligée-green leaves,
past that, past the olive mill's iron gear,
its cog wheel a useless, stationary thing
in a garden. At the hidden stairs I waited.
If I climbed the seven steps and unlatched
the picket gate, which green room
once entered would change my life?
I stayed below with the lime tree's green,
its fruit in early ripening, that tone,
and the cypress's and the persimmon's, too,
its fruit in full sun still half red,
half apple-green, neighbor to the wall
where morning glories bloom, their vine-y
green heightened by their one-day blue.
Near the bougainvillea a clay jug rested
with two great baskets and a watering
hose curled like a sleeping snake, allowed
to be a part of the garden's green shade,

to be a part of the garden's green shade,
a fragrance emerges from the past
and floats into the future I'll leave
behind, sometimes Lorca's horse
in the mountain, *el caballo en la montaña*,
the way green runs in spring
coming upon the peasant, making her
look up from the back gate. What
a surprise if a painting in mimicry
were true to the olive's or the lime tree's
tough green, its solidity a fortress-heavy

color, a house of the undomesticated,
even in winter's skeletal frame, a time
borne, splattered with blood, the traces
of red in a leaf's wings and veins,
the ghost of summer's weeks, visitor
to fruit and jug, basket and hose,
the absence that steals into a house
in September.–The lord of green
says nothing, but his heart has been moved.

Fisher's Club

A roadside inn. Lakeside dive. Spiffed up.
End of a summer day. And I suppose
I should be smiling beneficently
at the families playing near the shore,
their plastic balls and splashes and chatter.

But my eye pivots left to a couple;
he is carrying her into the water.
He's strong enough, and she is light
enough to be carried. I see
how she holds her own, hugging
his neck, his chest steady as his arms.

I have never seen such a careful dunk,
half-dunk, as he gives her. That beautiful
play he makes lifting her from the water.

And I suppose I should be admiring
the sunset, all purple and orange and rose now.
Nice porch here, too. Yeah, great view.

But I have never seen such a loving
as he gives her. Imagine
being so light as to float
above water in love.

Chance

Right at the worst time of your life someone
helps you in some way. And you have nothing
in your heart to pay them back. You must
take the least shred of it in, like some
huge gulping machine. Say it was
not human help, rather help from another
creature, totally oblivious of you, an owl, say,
a low call one evening from a winter bare tree.
And that was enough, enough to fill your ear
before you slept. Say you were
that desperate. How could you repay an owl
that you'd overheard, busy being owl?
But now you're better, stronger, a bit of the old
toughness reigns inside again, though you want
to keep that sharp awareness
pain left behind because you feel
you can never live, though
you do live, without these ragged
occasions some call chance.

Once, Late on a December Afternoon

on the corner of Thomas and Dale,
a lilac bush hosted a thousand sparrows,
their chatter, a way of keeping warm.
I heard them after a mass for the dead
I lived through by memorizing the altar,
the marble floor's inlaid patterns,
the priest crisscrossing them, his black
polished shoes, the polished malachite.

On my right stood a wooden creche, a joy
geared to the mystery of earth's animals
and heaven's angels meeting in a barn;
their hearty singing over the manger,
the priest singing over the casket. Yes.
That is what happened, its exact length.

little eternities

2015

"Time has always been the greatest wonder for me. Why is it now, but not then?" –Bai Hua

Time Traveler

You are leaving
or arriving.
All the same
in deep time.

Paleolithic,
Pharaonic,
outer galactic
or old Gallic,

all the same
in deep time.

In your place
you are here
today.

You can film it,
you can pin it
down in ink,
you can try but

no one's seen it
like you've seen it.
I have seen you
in your jacket

once a robe
on an ancient
Hittite tablet.

Summer of 2013

I was there. I always
wanted to live in 1913
and it came again,
a hundred years late,
but otherwise punctual
as a trombone slide
wandering slowly to
the accompaniment of
a brushed snare drum,
sh sh sh sh, feeling a bit
loose around the shoulders.
What time is

it anyway?–A train's
just pulled in, with
its chain of dark green
washed-to-gray *wagon lit*.
Steam breath
fouls the station's air.
A chugging hiss
makes it hard to hear
if someone's calling
to the young woman
in the train window.

Whether to the future or the past?

*

Give me another date.
1979.
I was there. Another.
2030.
Not invited yet.

There's a yearning hovering
around like Russian roulette.

*

Now the young woman's slipping
on her good brown pumps.
Now she's sliding off
the worn plush bench and
stands in the train car's door.
She surveys the platform's
crowd and then, nudged
by the minute and a passenger
behind her, she steps down.

If I Bend to Pick You Up

O! On my front stoop, hopping, a little sparrow.
Of all the birds in the world, you come to me, Sparrow.

You limp, you hobble. I can't help you though I want to;
I know nothing of fixing the flight of sparrows.

If my knees could bend, I'd scoop you up,
put you in a cardboard box, keep you safe, Sparrow.

You're just a sparrow after all, a common sparrow.
I'm not expected to take care of sparrows.

Your wing flutters, telling me what's wrong. I'm
the useless one. Physician, how do you heal a sparrow?

If he's to be mine after I unlock the front door,
he will be disappointed, whether man or sparrow.

Out of panic? fear? a last chance? you come so close
to my shoes, one-half inch more and—the tap of a sparrow.

Are you that humble to tap my foot?
Or does height mean nothing to a sparrow?

All I can offer is the shelter of my garden patch.
You retreat. I do not feel good about this, Sparrow.

Yes, stay there for tonight's storm, under the mugo pine.
Peck among seeds, the only food I have for sparrows.

Words may work on paper but they have the weight
of snow-grit which you may not see this year, Sparrow.

I'm so sorry. What if I die first? And death is so
untrustworthy. I, Sharon, could return as cat, Sparrow.

I Won't Turn on the Radio

rather I'll listen to the rain,
a rich companion promising
mutual benefits.

After a drought or long absence,
the god of rain can be steady
or scary. Chaque/ Tlaloc to the South.

Thor's thunder from the North.
I love them both. Some nights
love can be desperate

as well as passing.
Mine bears no grudges
against rain's music,

its artful way in bed
leading the listener
to sleep's side.

Size

I was in a dress shop that ranked sizes 3 to 0,
    0 being a size where even robins
loom large, where the rest of the world is

a snow field 0-woman slogs through daily, taking
    her small heart in tow, whispering
to it, *Courage, courage*, the way the French

pronounce a singingly low-pitched chocolaty vowel—
    ahzh! —which soothes
the size-rage a small American may feel. A petty

thought if the 0-woman is a black belt in Karate
    or a Sunday schooler
or Yeshiva student studying David and Goliath,

or "Small Is Beautiful" like social justice Catholics,
    though that never was
as successful in Guatemala as "Black Is Beautiful"

in Chicago and was subsumed in the early 21st century
    by Hummer-like Big Business
and rashes of heartlessness. Remember *The Glass*

Menagerie, those frail figures, how they crouched
    when Jim entered the room?
Their only chance to hide away was to be over-

looked, to never ask a total stranger for a kiss
    out of loneliness in a city
of complications so beyond miniature it's more

like a minotaur heart devourer. Everything
    snaps when the little
heart is swallowed or must be squirreled away

like the family silver from invaders. 'Heartless'
    can burn like a million
tiny red hearts sucked on O-woman's tongue.

Thyme

Old, single-syllable word with an old-fashioned *th* beginning, an ancient consonant-compound that lodges back of front teeth and turns an h under tongue-pressure into common *ta* to usher out a quaint Y, sounding just like long i today.—A trick older than a hand-made lace collar that startles the dark bodice it circles. Elegant in form, Y is as totally at home mid-word as a tool in its chest. And neighbor to M, a favorite human sound which floats away with the silent *e*. A miracle the *e* hasn't been dropped; it's a gnomic little happiness defending the presence of the useless. A tale in nothingness. Whether recognized or not, the e hangs on for dear life. Inaudible as fragrance. Maybe carrying an important message from the halls of silence.

L'Arlésienne: Madame Joseph-Michel Ginoux, Van Gogh, 1888-89

> *"These hard features were once soft, and these cold,
> almost malicious eyes were friendly and innocent."*
> —Robert Walser, Looking at Pictures

But she's pretty, Herr Walser. Look again.
You don't like the single line that leads
at the same time up to a curved eyebrow
and down to rosebud lips? Or her famed
lady-like table posture, resting her cheek
on her big hand, a useful hand
that's seen its share of gutting geese
and dusting off a book? She may stumble
over a word, back up and start again
but she can read.

                Maybe, Herr Walser,
you misjudged the ambition in her eyes?
She's happily obliged to wear her best,
her Sunday dress, a navy with a pale
scarf. She's primped a bit combing
her dark satiny hair. She's wet her fingers
to set her bangs in spit curls. Just so
on the forehead. And pat into place a navy
matron's cap with scarf-tail. Just so

she sits in the painting for hours, years,
never hearing a demand for tea or lunch.
She's busy dreaming, Herr Walser,
on a week day no less, dreaming herself
into Madame L'Arlésienne who's seen
the world outside of Arles: Each morning in Paris
she heard a bright scale of tones,
Bonjour, Madame. Bonjour, Madame.
This souvenir welcomes her to all the time
in the world, even to herself at the table
with three books, one open, two waiting.

219

Eye Hole (eagpyrel=eye)

Not to be confused with window, the wind's eye. So many scenes pass by. Look what we walk through! An image climbs in and then climbs out, followed by galloping thought. Only a film maker can keep up. At the wedding dance, how it felt to have the skirt blooming at thigh level. And how it felt to move in close to the other's chest. This may feel so good you close your eyes. The eye hole can't feel like your arms and breasts can; its god-like power is limited, demanding light, blinking at darkness, maybe even threatened by it, scared by the thought of non-existence. How long did life on earth have to wait before eye holes evolved? Some priest somewhere knows exactly within ten thousand years.

    A compromise on dress straps ended the cold war between one priest and a bride. You see, her bridesmaids' dresses, cranberry-colored with a black ribbon for a belt, were strapless. Not whorish, in spite of the priest's insistence the shoulders be covered. (His nose holes, a-flare; wrath inside those hairy tunnels.) Oh, bosoms! Some eyes like to follow you, finding silhouettes and full fronts beautiful and sexy, and others want you hidden under dishtowels. Consider how old this conflict is. 1500 years ago the word for 'eye' was *eagpyrel*. How long before that did we wait before we could see blindness? An eye doesn't know. Still, it's so valuable it comes with its own protective lid. Well. This is how eternity works, so far.–Swallows rise and fly, dip in and out of a cliff's craters that look very much like the dark eye holes in Argus's skull.

On Milton's Political Pamphlets and the Measure of Time

> "London, Printed by Mathew Simmons, next dore
> to the gilded Lyon in Aldersgate Street, 1649."

As if the gilded Lyon would always be next dore,
ready to direct a writer's steps to the ancestor
of photocopiers near Aldersgate's homely glamour—
a fading Lyon. (A sign above a pub's door?
A statue, its gilt fading?) The present is so
strong in its little day-by-day affairs, bringing
down its lions somedays seems impossible.
Simmon's client Milton, for example, hiding
on a straw bed of fleas under a common, stale
coverlet.—Oh, a republic had seemed so
possible, buoyed on the stream of his pamphlets
arguing against a monarch's so-called sacred
calling. It seemed the civil war had ended
the dispute as if it wouldn't recur, in England
or elsewhere. As if *dore* could never be
spelled door. As if life couldn't be summed up
as an immense series of changing cruelties,
preserving, somewhat, a tittle of civility:
for appearance sake Milton's Parlimentarians
sewed King Charles's chopped-off head
back on for one last public display. (Using
horse hair or wire for thread?) But
the inscrutable *That Is* intrudes. Charles II
ascends the throne and Milton goes underground.
Try understanding this when the world's in upheaval,
and you have only a bit of lead to hold onto—
oh, the printer's clever fingers—one bit
for each letter in a word that, heavens! stays put.

The Tsarina's Tea Set

> Museum of Russian Art, Minneapolis

Incredible the Bolsheviks didn't smash it,
token of the Tsarina and the wild-eyed
Rasputin, who accidentally on purpose could've
ground a porcelain cup in his teeth
and not bled, proving to her his powers,

grinning and chomping down the delicate
painted birds on the cup, its background
a robin's egg blue or the tint in a woman's
bedroom wallpaper.—Swallow-like birds
I can't name, their own invincible magic

flown from a brush's dash-dash, o,
trickle-down, tangible happiness, the royal
that escaped assassination. O happy little
birds, happy blue teapot boxed in a museum's
vitrine. You'll be the family that lasts forever.

A Life With the Movies

Not too much, is it, to ask from a week—
Tuesday. *Night of the Iguana*. Tequila.
I'd hate to drink to nothing at all.

Wednesday, *The Northwest Passage* to Friday,
I lift my glass to the empty chair beside me.
Not too much, is it? To ask from a week?

Thursday is totally *Mutiny on the Bounty*.
I mix a Titanic: drink three and you're sunk.
I'd hate to drink nothing at all.

Chicago. Valentine's Day. Al Capone. Still
bloody alone. Calls for a double shot.
Not too much to ask from a week. Is it

Saturday? *Dinner at Eight*. 1933. I'm late.
Sunday's *Love in the Afternoon* is a boring fling.
I hate to drink to nothing. After all

Father Knows Best. Monday is a light white
wine, sipped for all the *Miss Lonely Hearts*.
Not too much to ask, is it, from a week
of drinking to nothing at all? That I'd hate.

One Has to Say

some numbers are so old they were first
counted on thumbs, long before humans
described numbers with names and pinned
one's solitary status down, in times when
the potter in his hut never went beyond
a surplus of two. Demands for more
yielded stick markings in the yard's dirt
to show 'how much.' And maybe nouns
stepped in then, the equivalent of our own
"a lot," "a bunch."—How many warriors?
As many as the villagers in the valley.
Accumulation wanted exactness though.
Beyond ten, fingers struggled with the weight
to be more than a bone-creaking abacas;
hands, more than a carousel of counting.
The brainy wanted squaring and pairing
and leapt figuratively from the finger's first
knuckle toward the mind's imagined pi.—All
the while that old, lovely chaos, Zero in her room,
rocking in her chair, chuckled, holding her offsprings'
feet to the ur deca-system, the hands' original frame.

For the Millions Who Were Starved to Death in Ukraine

   the Holodomor, 1932-33, a man-made famine

In the Lands of Et Cetera and the recurring Et Al where
genocides come and go, will be and have been, ordered
on a timetable by the emperor of madness,
          a footpath
through a field leads to the hollow where a body
collapsed and its life passed, a life that in the afterwards
continues in saved letters and rumors

    "...and a man cannot endure this for a long time.
There are eight in our family..."
         "... have sent to Poland
all the clothes we could sell for food."
    She ate her baby?
–He would've died anyway.

        The clothes chest, empty.
The grass, picked clean. Insects and birds, long ago eaten.

The 900 Pound Man, the Fattest in the World

He did not wear shoes, had no shoes,
for no shoes fit his monstrous feet
or held his monstrous weight. And besides
he didn't need shoes in bed.
                        Nor do
caterpillars in their cocoons, devouring
every hour on their way to butterfly (while he ate
he felt light).
                   He did not wear pants,
not as we know pants. His were sheets, sewn
half way up the middle? And for a shirt,
a third sheet cut like a poncho?
                   Who

could gather him in their arms, who
could get close enough to meet his lips,
drawn and thin–
          His eating

was a longing to stop time?–He lost

six hundred pounds, had to pick up
his loose flesh to walk or shove a leg
into pants. A chattering pack of hounds–
blue-gloved nurses and surgeons–
met at his boundaries and filleted away
bags-full of flesh, saving
        the capillaries, bloody little
        creeks running right under
        the epidermis, peripheries
        he must not lose.

    Just think,

the 900 pound man ate farther into
oblivion than any human ever
on this planet. His weight, the tiny
country he'd made for himself.

The Wounded Angel

> painting, Hugo Simberg, 1903

This happened long ago when blood
root bloomed, the dazed spring still
holding onto makeshift railings.

We sloshed around winter's old fields
in poor man's shoes, bought large
to grow into. We heard the stubble

breathe *caution, caution,* saw
something white crumple and fall
from the sky. A heron? Wild swan?

 We ran toward it. A wingéd thing,
a heap of feathers we carried home,
her feet too odd for any shoes.

That was the year an angel lived
in our kitchen, recuperating
on the bench beside Mother's oven.

She isn't like us, Mother said,
when we're tired or hurt.
She won't put up any fuss.

That was the year we learned
about earth and its gravities,
how they hold some of us

down, but free the unearthly.
From the kitchen's back stoop
we three watched the angel

unfurl her wings one morning
and barefoot, take flight
into the blue heaven we call sky.

Re The Art of Painting/ *De Schilderkonst* 1666-68/ Jan Vermeer

Wanting at least two sets of eyes, his
and his reflection's, Vermeer
devised contraptions
                like mirrors–
rear views of himself,
broad back and billowing bottom–
                        in a room
where a huge wall map
           was a link
                to the North Sea.

De Noord See. The world. Its ships,
big as bugs
                where he, or I, on deck
could look out
        through imagination's
                      spyglass
                            and see,
really see

the only thing
alive that counts
on a perfect June evening

is gathering
        surface & light
                with longing
and introducing them
        like destined lovers
                to each other.

A Small Repast of Tea and Kippers

One day I shall swim away like a herring,
he said.
And be eaten like a fish by death,
she said.
At high tea, high tide; she
pours, he divides the fish.

She asked what was that noise
outside.
He thought it a loose shingle,
flapping.
They both heard his belly,
growling. Later, the sea

calmed down. Murmured, she said.

Mister Miłosz, Aprés Party

> *"Aï, my dead of long ago! Aï, Hanusevich, aï, Nina!*
> *Nobody remembers you, nobody knows about you ....*
> *He (Mister Hanusevich) caroused with chanteuses, pretending*
> *to be a big shot,*
> *Would send a telegram in Russian, 'Arriving with ladies*
> *Meet with music troikas champagne ...'*
> *And a signature: Count Bobrinskii."*
>
> – from "Mister Hanusevich" by Czesław Miłosz

I was there, too, though I am here, Miłosz. I'm the good girl, was the good girl in the back of the restaurant by the door. I volunteer to tell how you pulled on your brown leather jacket, sleeve by slippery satin-lined sleeve, how the evening was classy, arrogant, expensive, how the big bill waved unpaid in Uncle Innkeeper's hand as we left, laughing, waiting for the troika that came late. (Nina's patent leather shoes got soaked.) That night was like all nights staked out for us. Though I wasn't there, I am there in a nerdy, literary twist on the Ruthian promise "Wherever you go, I will go," following Mr. Hanusevich, et al, all bedfellows on paper, midge-y shadows that bugged your hand, tagged along as you write.Wrote. It's questionable you'll ever read this, lying as your body does in a crypt on a familiar Kraków street. Who knows. But you made that night, like all nights, bloom for the spangle-hatted and gutsy, the great pretenders, the big-shot high rollers, the champion champagne cork poppers, the Count Bobrinskiis from the confiscated country estates, the most boozy of all the angels.

p.s. I love how you shrug, so your jacket: or a phrase: fits: hangs: just right.

Starry Nights of Pantry Labor

"I was born very far from where I'm supposed to be, so I'm on my way home." Bob Dylan

Maybe soulscape begins as door.
        Your hand, hesitant on the handle,

not sure where you'll feel at home.
        Yours won't come looking for you.

A sea rushes in only so far. Deserts demand
        you stumble onto them.

The search is a little like flirting, like
        the flirting between Jesus

and the Samaritan woman at the well,
        her oasis in an arid land

where they prattled on, each sharing
        their thoughts on water.

Sometimes you follow the harsh back
        of winter to find the soul

scape that matches you. It may happen
        on a starry night of pantry labor:

what is missing, what is at hand.
        Light streams in, wave after wave

moves through your rooms,
        traversable mountains.

Little Eternities

An energetic but murky mating in the bog–
frogs thick in the muck, no leg-room between,

not like patio chairs arranged to stand
apart from each other, not like families

separated by miles or rage, not like ghosts
of those long gone, rather like crowding

into a blinding urge to dwell intensely.
Look at shimmering leaves in sunlight,

they never move alone. Unless you remember
autumn's last leaf dangling from a branch.

But you won't, in spring you won't favor
a clan of faded ladies. I, too, dead-head

to abet the next blossom.–Once
I walked in a field of peonies, of every color

and ruffled petal. Blue dragonflies also visited.
The rain had stopped and the sun hadn't yet

unleashed its strongest beat. Thus around noon
for long moments, we were all together.

The J Horoscope

2019

"Now look: man becomes a creature of flesh." *The Book of J*

Intersection #1

Mango. The color surprised us, flew
over us in the eye of a bird, in feathers.
We couldn't get enough of it.

Not salmon, not tangerine. Mango.
It turned our teeth pink.
Each laugh was a bite of it.

We left hatred behind for mango.
Even blame, which we couldn't
let go of

quite, even our blame
drummed mango,
mango to our ears.

We danced to mango
close like lovers. Mango's
sweetness melted us into life.

Yahweh the Stork

I've seen it all—the father who killed his son,
the sons who threw their brother down a well,
the father-in-law who ordered his son's wife
burned to ash, it's happened under orange roofs
on this very street where nary a wind stops.
From the town's light pole, my nesting place,
I watch a kid on the curb, kicking stones,
yearning for something more, like new relatives,
though if they arrive, park their blue car
at the front gate, tumble out, helloing, spilling
their stories and habits all over the living room,
they'll truss the kid up with their family ties.
The next day I deliver another baby, a bundle
of trust; yes, babies have to trust, that's the first
unspoken contract with the world. The first forgotten.

The Boatman's Wife

She spent mornings corralling the stupid hen.
All for eggs. Not one thought
about whacking off the hen's head and
serving chicken for dinner ...

           In the aviary
birds shivered watching her search
nests they had with difficulty hidden.

She wished she could shit like a bird
before taking off and fly straight out
of this whole mess.
                In storms,
bailing out the boat or hunting down
loose snakes, she longed for books

left on her shelf at home: Joseph Campbell,
James George Frazer.
                      Thinkers! Unlike
the Boatman, who believed every damned
rain drop was prophecy,

                throwing his head back,
gulping rain down, letting his beard grow
long and ratty.
                He numbered the days
in charcoal marks on the walls,
his thick glasses steamy with sweat.

Evenings he fashioned tiny Eves
from rib bones.
                She never
should've married him. Penned in
for the rest of her houseboat life.

How long would that last? At least
she could save the birds.
At least, this one dove—

The Cuckold's Dream

You see the power of a dream, one dream
that explains why pain and the devil exist
in this lopsided paradise. You see how one
dream cradles crow and sacrifice. You see
in a dream's proselytizing how manna's
image hardens into generations of bread.

I listen to the why, the good that makes
what is mysterious about us, which is
a story's direction, leading from one thing,
plunging back at will to cover complications,
like the pure, fragrant joy found in eating
with your woman. I forget everything for flavor.

Luck Out for a Walk

Maybe a long afternoon. Maybe rain the challenge.
It pops an umbrella up for the underpopulation.

Maybe a place to hide. In a crowd Garbo
never wanted her face seen either,
too many people stopping, wanting favors.

Luck's own round world. Stylish black. The handle,
a shepherd's crook turned crook-curve down.

She loves rain's thrum on satin. Old fashioned.
Socially acceptable like an arm to hold onto.
Maybe her man catches up,

ducks under.
Until the downpour lifts then—

Dove with Hint of Green Backs

Toward evening as on Fridays
when the heart sings,
and the eagle flies,
a little note dangles
from the dove's beak.

Words in black ink
run with the magic
a bank can cash. Dear bird,
I thrill, so
relieved to read of your nest.

THESE EARTHLINGS MAY HAVE SEEN YAHWEH

          personals from the *Babel Tower Gazette*

1.
My purse was open on a chair,
an old man shambled toward me, an old purse snatcher,
an old there's-fresh-fish-for-supper smile on his face.
Was it him?
        Small Fry

2.
I Hear That Lonesome Whistle,

            whoo-ooo-oo.

Hey, Good Looking!

           I'm So Lonesome I Could Cry

Why Don't You Love Me?

           Like You Used to Do?

You were my thrill.

        B. Hill

3.
Dam or damsel?
          Puzzled

4.
He gives me three, small bells.
For my garden, he says, for my door, and the table beside my bed.
Call me, he says.
          Girl Next Door

5.
A red apple. Once perfect now
one cheek missing. The bite that hurt.
                              Ms. Snake

6.
So he wears a suit. So what? So does
the jeweler, hunched in his little, frayed shop.
                              FB Post

7.
How can a day already have passed?
I have done nothing, nothing.
Tsk. Pardon, my confusion.
It's only me, lounging in the sun.
                              Chrysanthemum

Ms. Yahweh in P.S. #1

When they began that cloysome, fond calling—
Yahweh?—I didn't know them. It was fall,

I hadn't a seating chart or a lesson plan.
They'd soon smell it out, my lack of planning,

their noses keen as animals'. A dog's. A doe's.
I asked the round-faced boy in the window row

for his name, and the girl, very small for 7th grade,
in front of him. She dug inside her binder, laid

a notebook on her desk, pointed to a sentence in
a cosmos-sized story about names

that couldn't be hers. Just tell me what you want
to go by in school, I said. She actually panted.

How could this be so difficult? While I waited
for her name, the class tottered to their fate,

the wildness of the undisciplined and lost,
a frolic-y panic, the instinctive and natural chaos

in children, like a late summer storm in the yard
when all gains are lost in the apple yield.

Flies, Theology 1.

Gawd,
how the flyswatter
hates flies.

Flies, Theology 2.

Gawd, how
a flyswatter
loves a fat
fly.

.

INTERSECTION # 8

Looking for someone who'd like to be in a REAL NSA relationship. This is for real, let's talk and meet. You'll love my eager piercing eyes. I'm a man of the world. I love to kiss and deep subjects. Money's no problem. I like to do things rather than just talking about it, and there's a lot to do out here. I'm a little shy at first, but WOW, after I open up, I'm very fun to be with.

p.s. Only virgins need apply.

The Family Album

Over the years, so many days;
who can remember them all?

Walls bulge, windowsills swell
with the past. Children, popped

from the same, small pod, fly off
in different directions to work,

marriage; work, death. Goodness,
back into closed closets!

There's always the book, the drawer
that exists to be opened. And hands

of girls, comely, or only comely
in the dark, passed on in marriage

like the deed to the family cabin.
Think needlepoint. Think green

and blue stitching. On the wall,
framed, Old Aunt Tamar's saying:

The first place he enters
is your arms. All your battles

take place on the bloody plain
between your two dusky legs.

Yahweh the Stork re Mother One Heart

She's the tree the two hung from, suckling her plump,

ripe breasts, pushing their noses into her fleshy bags.

Mother of twins, she thanked me for the gift, raising

her hands, palms up—(Hear? The despairing sigh

among leaves?)—but is this what she'd prayed for?

One would've done, she said. And not the first born,

the rugged one his father loves, rather the second,

born to paint her portrait, his dark, sensitive eyes

flashing from the canvas to her pose: A tree,

a spreading tree, powerfully smelling sweet.

A tree with his initials heart-carved into the trunk.

A tree bent over the years from sheltering her

foxy son. As he speeds away in her lustrous black

Audi, she always waves, *Be home for supper, Love?*

To Joseph the Dreamer, the Pretty Boy

> "A many-colored coat was made for Joseph. His brothers grasped that it was him their father loved most; they hated him, could not speak warmly to him...'Look, here comes our master of dreams,' the brothers said among themselves. 'Now is a time to kill him, then throw him down an abandoned well.'" #78 & 81, pp. 118-9, The Book of J.

You're driven from your land to another.
This isn't what you planned, to live
as a foreigner, an exile drumming up work.
But you are wild and lovely, as common
as a broom. You learn to speak in many
tongues. Their words flame in your mouth.
Your kiss falls with the lightness of a bee.
Your smile is real not carved. Not like
a jack-o-lantern's crooked, botox smile.
In the land of Egyptians and Canadians
the intelligence of your light is sung.
Or: Many envy you. Envy we now know
is madness. Be nimble, Joseph.
     Be quick.
        Jump—

  *

Be nimble. Be quick. Jump—
       They,
your jealous brothers, half-brothers,
will sell you. They threaten to wash
your suck-up mouth out with sheep shit.
They throw you down a well. You writhe
into the evening under the Sea of Crisis.
Father howls at the moon, Come home, Son.
The thing is, you never really wanted to
live in this world. Your mother would've
taken any child, but she had you. You
came out the same place your father slid

in. (O, wonder, one that employs her
for the rest of her days.) She is your
door to this world under the moon.

*

A door to this world under the moon
opens in dreams. What you can't grasp
by day is do-able in sleep. Deep
in the east, the mind does its drama
drudge-work, running for miles,
counting years of famine like cows,
finding the path up from the bottom
of a well. If you dream long enough,
someone's bound to come along,
ears itching to tell a riddle, a tiny stage
morphing from lectern to mountain,
rock to elevator, from stove to bell to tree.
No one needs insight; a dream wrestles
for you. All you must do is interpret.

*

All you must do is interpret
why they, your eleven half-brothers,
(not to mention a half-sister) get nothing
but chores. It's not hard to figure out,
conceived as you were by the new
woman your father is besotted with.
Because it never stops, how you get
whatever they want most: a gift
from their Dad like the coat, pure
cashmere, that Father bought for you.
And when a box arrives, a delivery seen
from their mother's, the First Wife's, measly,
second-rate window, it lands in Joseph's
arms. No wonder they want to kill you.

*

No wonder they want to kill you.
You own their very dreams, taking up
the whole bed as you slide, REM
time, into a dream's glade, your hand
gun loaded with retribution. Yes,
you blast away at will. Who's worse,
you ask the bears in dream parlance,
the hoodwinker or the hoodwinked?
In the birch bark silence, X is the bully
you conquer. He/she/they bother
you no more. Your mind makes you
a rich man to boot. You leave the path
to the past littered with spent shells—
you're out of there. You wake happy.

*

You wake happy. The wind's swung
from south to north. The wheat's
shocked. The harvest, in. The drought
that famished many lands skipped
yours, an exile's fields, fat enough
for more and more, your granaries
bursting. Your brothers, rain-starved,
ten hats on the hooks in your hall,
arrive to bum wagons of wheat off you.
Thoughts storm in from all directions.
Memories tumble wild over grass land.
This is how one grievance is wiped out:
a family gathers on the front porch,
everyone rushes in to escape the rain.

*

Everyone rushes in to escape the rain
like a man running into a promise

that may be a cage. You stay close
to the door and keep it unlocked for
hurried departures. The strangest thing,
in the interim you've grown old.
While aiming at futures? Subtracting
and adding up figures in rows of years?
You don't know. What's important?
Your window breathes light and brilliant
use of shadow. Outside, some talk among
the oaks, not in words of course but in shade
and interval, a little like one of your dreams
where you're driven from your land to another.

INTERSECTION #6

We were at the intersection
between Sodom and Gomorrah.
We were at the interstice of knowing
how far God would go, we were
testing Him to see how fast He'd race
away from us, 0 to 60 in two seconds,
how soon He'd freak out at our worst,
even as we knew He'd let at least one
swallowtail escape, one transparent,
winged innocent elude damnation.
He'd give it time to flutter away
before He blew up the rest of us
sucked oranges, we who by nature
will do anything to fly high.

Lost in Love

Once an owl flew into the tree's
other, leafy city. I was beyond you,
beside myself, barely breathing.

I didn't turn on a light, didn't move
from my shadow. I was wanting
the god calling outside the window,

the One Voice,
the lovely Who-who-
who circles the moon's horn.

The Gardener in Eden

He sat in a lawn chair while his neighbor
the scribe ghost-wrote his memoir.

This was in the days before birds and feathers.
Only wind and snakes were heard in trees.

Make it tart, Henry, the gardener mused.
Make the woman dangle from the story line.

Stories curled over their gray heads like pipe smoke,
a shroud dissipating into the garden's topiary.

*The female was a temptress. And remember
she listened to a snake. Dissed me.*

It was autumn, the ground hardened with apples,
the deers' winter stock of apple fat.

Wasps searched gables and window sills.
The glade bee-loud, its roses tall as apple trees.

The gardener closed his eyes. *Make it sting, Henry.*
Henry sniggered. *And reward her with curse.*

The rain that night was spotty, raising an odor
of dust and the gardener's tight lips. This was

in the days before the garden's overgrown paths,
when the gardener's roof tiles still held fast.

Yahweh the Cook's Opinion

Had the man asked for the moon, his mother
would have found some way to pull it down,
all the while asking what else she could do.

Never would she send him so far away
as outer space, for how could she bear
her house if he were the night's cold face

smiling down on her?—I keep my hands
out of their intrigues. Are her woes
worth my while? Does she pay me for wits?

She pays me to cook. To keep the kitchen
orderly and the food smelling scrumptious.
Sometimes I joke. She frowns. Her son,

the tease, nips at my ear. But things could be a lot
happier around here if she'd learn, as I have,
she can never fix the distance between them.

Eve's Daughter Marilyn

A piece of work—those bought and hung
in the gallery where SHE studied resemblances
between Picasso's jar and Roy Lichtenstein's,
Picasso's mistress and Jasper John's. She,
understanding an iota about the masters.

Face me. Look beautiful. Big smile now.
Let me see you without the blouse on.

Listen: She snubbed them. In that ravishing way
blonds have when the gallery guard is watching. *Little*
jack horner sat in a corner... his mouth dropping
open ... *eating his curds and whey* ..., reaching
for his pocket (*he stuck in his thumb and pulled*
out a ...) blackberry? (*What a good boy am I!*)

In dazzling, spiked heels, she paused for full
effect over the floor vent, her white skirt
aswirl around two long, tanned lovelies.
All eyes in heaven bugged at her masterpiece.
It was the beginning of the world.

CAIN

We loved Harleys, the speed, the air in hair,
the gangs & gin & guns. On the road again.

And Mom? Laughing. "I've created a man,
just like God." My bro and I were gods?
Or she was? She was funny that way.

Anyway, The Family Innocent got shot in a fight
with me over a girl. Not very respectable

when one son kills the other. And Adam-Dad?
Pretty defeated by then, always in danger
of apoplexy. Go ahead, he used to goad me,

bring more shame on our name.
Well, I tried my best, and I won.

The First Old Woman to Have an Egg Planted Between Her Legs

> "Within her, Serai's (Sarah's) side split: 'Now that I'm used to groaning, I'm to groan with pleasure? My lord is also shriveled." #41, p. 82, The Book of J.

Not that she didn't look at men, especially young men, the shirtless gardener, his nice, muscly chest, curvy brown shoulders, flat tummy caving down to the hairy place where the cock crows mornings, stirring and sweet. How old was she, having these seventh grade fantasies. He, her husband, had been up to all of them when they were young. You can't get pregnant from a wink though, which is about all she'd get from the gardener. She was old, for heaven's sake, groaning with arthritis; to be truthful, fearful: how would her bones hold up under the load of a man? But she had a dream and couldn't shake it. Why not make use of science? Didn't it promise a longer life? Cures? Babies? All the things she once prayed for. Clear skin, shiny hair. All you need today is money, a good doctor, an insurance plan, cheaper, if you're rich, than God who demands a tithe. Who'd want a kid when she's sixty, some of her friends, grandmothers all, asked. Was it wise? When you're seventy, they'd clucked, the kid'll only be ten! Wise-schmise. She wanted her dream lying red-faced and nibbling at her nipple. On the day the magic happened, for all the neighbors to see, she'd have a diaper run up the front yard's flag-pole, followed by her red, double-A bra. You fly.

Yahweh the Avenger

One day a girl prayed to me, "You know,
this place used to be cool. Lots of parties.
Now I think you should nuke it."

Cities of light zapped into glitz and tinsel.
A man like Beethoven was lucky,
stuck in deafness, not catching the chaos.

Hear the violins' tremolo over the ruins?
My chilled angels. All things once loved–

the Rhenish pitcher, the Dürer rabbit–
sometimes I remember them with sadness.

Yahweh the Rock

They never loved me. They never even liked me.
People prayed for a rock, and I was it.
And then I wasn't because they wanted me
to be like them: move, shout, scream,
show some spasm of expression. A rock?
What they missed, once they were alone
in a shack in the desert, in a cabin or bankrupt
on a mountain, what they missed was a rock's
steadfastness, made of mineral, made of earth.
Humans waver, un-rock-like. No heft and girth …
but pleasing palms! I like to lie in their shallows.
And I like to fly like a brick hurled against a tank
or skip swallow-like across a lake, or clatter
down a hill's scree into a guileless place.
A couple finds me. "This one's lucky," they say.
"Let's keep it forever." Frankly, very few do.

WHERE ONE BECOMES TWO

The old fox has died.
Now his mate is alone.
Now she must cross the river alone.

Look.
In the water.
Two foxes.

Yahweh the Stork Re a Human Condition

Flying through time and topography to shelter
I've heard it all from my nest on the stork pole.
A hundred-year-old woman conceives. A teen
gets pregnant but remains a virgin. Both have sons,
fuel for sacrifice. A knife blade through the chest
awaits one; torture, the other. The first saved
by a moment, the second nailed to a gallows
like a bloodied sack of millet. Stories! The night's
and a god's glut. Human kind swallows them
the way a hungry stork swallows a frog. In one tale
a gawky troupe of two servants, a boy and his
old man climb the mountain Jehovah-jireh.
In the second, the pregnant virgin rocks toward
Bethlehem on a donkey.–The Gauls and Saxons,
Greeks and Egyptians, Horites, Hyksos,
Swahilis and Anasazi, Tuaregs, Persians, Incas,
Anishinaabeg, and Mongolians make their own tales
from egg and sperm. That old Hebrew sheepman,
his face dripping with sweat, felt pressed into
off-ing his son. A knife aimed at the heart.
The moment on the mountain passed, and a voice
that sounded very much like his wife's rang out, *Enough!*

The Host

Like a farmer undone
        by bounty, bushed just thinking about the next
wheelbarrow load of radishes and zucchinis, she
        pins her mane
                back into a knot and calls for light.
Light for her table. The table's blue lamp emboldens
                platters of milky, husked corn, sheeny-green
peppers, the sausages' splatter–

        Bratsblutandknockwurstweisswurstleberwurst
        kielbasasaucissesalchichasosijipemmican–dozens

            of links and bags recorded in ledgers until
            the host covers her ears.

                              Did you know

        the sausage maker begat the pastry maker;
        the hunter, the fisher; the gardener,
        the florist; the spice maker, the canner,

        all preservers, all of long lineage, smock-wearers,
praisers of oceans and lakes, amen! gardens and prairies,

yes! *and* the horizon's order of dawn and evening

        imprinted on the hungry, the thirsty,
            the between-meals.

Let's eat!
        a raconteur shouts. The raconteurs,
prone to thirst, arrive first, full of pomp and eager
        to earn their supper. For as the host says,
        a story's light around a table
(made of wood the violin maker suggested)

         or a light story is good.
As is laughter. As is ardor.

It is said, and much hoped to be true,
the host overlooked not one soul. Amen.

Speaking in Riddles

2021

" ... what forces of the spirit do we need
blindly beating despair against despair
to ignite a spark a word of atonement ...

I don't know—my friend—and that's why
I send you these owl's riddles in the night ..."

—Zbigniew Herbert, "To Ryszard Krynicki—a Letter"

Seven Riddles:

It's hot. She squats on the curb, one elbow on
her knee, her hand dangling like a limp rag at the
end of a bone. When she talks to herself now and
then the rag flutters. (#69)

Using one of my agents—lamp or flare,,
metaphor or window—I wake you.
I am the master of arousal. Strong,
I can wake any creature. (#1)

Just one of them, pushed into your chest,
ain't a sign of love, Bub. A *Je t'accuse!* can precede
a firing squad or the preacher's wagging. Still
these bony ones can make a cashmere-soft
Come 'mere. Or discretely wipe a tear
or guide a nub across a paper. (#2)

You choose an orange tool for me
and then a red. Or a black. Whichever
sticks are beautiful to your eye
transform all things they rub against.
When you're done, please return them. (#15)

Back and forth it swings, not knowing
if it will be made to slam or click.
Its ball, a mirror-gleam in the dark.
It's ruled by a hole and a hinge and
a mantra: Open. Close. Hang. (#51)

Earthliness lies at the frame
of the east window. A breeze
becomes a mate to the room.
Thunder parks its bike away in a cloud,
and crickets jam a rondelet. (#7)

I am big and round. I'm cold or hot.
In my belly lie bones and beans,
skin or greens. Sometimes, tongue.
I'm at home with a spoon or, for that
matter, the knife. My freight's my goods;
they smell !good! and lure you to me.
When their savor is gone my belly's
empty again. (#17)

Solutions to Riddles:

Sun. This book begins with the sun. Call it *sigel*, *sol* or *Re*, imagine Earth without it. (#1)

Bag Lady (#69)

Fingers. A vital component to the language of the hearing impaired.
And actors.(#2)

A Box of Crayons. Or the crayons/ crayolas in it. (# 15)

A Door. (A member of the male body may also seem plausible.) (# 51)

A Summer Evening. Spending it at home, alone, is the impetus for this riddle. (#7)

A Pot/ Kettle/ Cauldron: Use of pots may be present in all cultures' DNA. (# 17)

Acknowledgments

Last but First: No acknowledgment page is complete without praising in gratefulness the many poets, teachers, listeners, editors, designers, publishers, copy editors, readers, and friends who have helped me along the way. And put up with me! I appreciate and thank you to no end. *Viva!*–

Sharon

The author happily acknowledges these zines for publishing the new poems or versions of them:
Burningword, "Waking at Night": also nominated for Burningword Prize; "We Missed the Boat"; *Askew*: "Keats Drops in on Wordsworth at Rydal Mount with His Friend Brown, 1819;"*Ekphrasis*: "City of Arhirit"; "Re the Tree Outside My Sink Window: Winter Spaces;"*Ascent*: "The Present Gives Up Some Past," "Five x Five Equals Two-Five;" "The Traveler;" "To Our Lady of the Snow," nom. for a Pushcart, 2017; *Miramar*: "Prayers Like Good Samaritans;" *Salt*: "Doesn't It Swell," "Photo of a Friend's Marsh in Winter;" *S.D. Pasque Petals*: "Eight Dakota Riffs on Rilke's 'Herbsttag' (Autumn Day)" First place, landscape category 2020 SD Poetry Society Award; *More on Time, a Tribute to Ted Kooser*: "Aunt B;" *Louisiana Literature*: "A Route from the Small;"*The Talking Stick*: "If I Could Write …"; "The People's Bakery;" *Oakwood*: "To Put My Finger on It"; "The Robin's Wife"; "Earthly Home"; "The Old Woman in Times of Aggression"; *North Dakota Quarterly*: "Stoves Go Well with Snow"

Journals That Have Published Poems from Books in This Collection under Occasionally Different Titles or Revisions: Milkweed Journal; Sing Heavenly Muse; Where One Voice Ends Another Begins; Borderlands; Cumberland Poetry Review; Ontario Review; Prairie Schooner; Room of One's Own; The Beloit Poetry Journal; Salmagundi; Lake Street Review; Rhino;

Slant; Ascent; Abraxis; Poetry Northwest; Spoon River Review; Poetry East; Barrow Street; Poet Lore; Minnesota Monthly; Exquisite Corpse; The Iowa Review; Cutbank Review; Notre Dame Review; Mid American Poetry Review; Margie, The American Journal of Poetry; The American Voice; The Seneca Review; The Chiron Review; Bearings; Water~Stone Review; The North Dakota Quarterly; The Briar Cliff Review; Speakeasy; Southern Poetry Review; North American Review; Ekphrasis; Phoebe SUNY-Oneonta; Turtle Quarterly; Whistling Shade;What Light; Dust & Fire; Loonfeather; Main Channel Voices; American Life in Poetry; Kritya, a Journal of Poetry; Nowa Okolica Poetów; Great River Review; St. Paul Almanac; Cider Creek Review; Anthology of 18 MN Poets; Pirene's Fountain; Solo Novo; Epoch; Contemporary American Voices; Commonweal; Conduit; Kestrel; Meditations on Divine Names; Lief; The Hudson Review; Pushcart Prize Nominations:1999, 2012, 2002, 2005, 2007, 2010, 2013, 2017, 2018, 2019

About the Author

Sharon Chmielarz was born and raised in Mobridge, South Dakota, but has spent her adult life in Minnesota. Her first two books, *Different Arrangements* and *But I Won't Go Out in a Boat* were awarded Minnesota Voices Prizes. Her book *The Other Mozart*, a biography in poetry, was made into an opera. Her collections *Visibility: Ten Miles* and *Speaking in Riddles* were finalists for the 2015 and 2021 Midwest Book Awards. *little eternities* was a finalist for the Ben Franklin Award. *Calling* and *The Widow's House* were finalists for the Next Generation Indie Books Awards. The latter, along with *The J Horoscope*, were named by *Kirkus Reviews* in the Best Books of 2016 and 2019.

    Chmielarz's work has been a finalist in the National Poetry Series, and her poems have been nominated several times for a Pushcart Prize. They have been featured on American Life in Poetry, and individual poems have been translated into French and Polish. She's the recipient of a Jane Kenyon Award from *The Water~Stone Review*. Her poems have been published in *The Notre Dame Review, The Iowa Review, Prairie Schooner, The Hudson Review, The North American Review, North Dakota Quarterly, Commonweal, Salmagundi, Margie, Salmagundi, The Seneca Review, Louisiana Literature, Ontario Review, CutBank*, and in Nodin Press's 2015 poetry anthology.